The Hypochondriac's Guide to Life. and Death.

GENE WEINGARTEN

With an Introduction by Dave Barry

Illustrations by Bob Staake

SIMON & SCHUSTER

SIMON & SCHUSTER
Rockefeller Center
1230 Avenue of the Americas
New York, NY 10020

SIMON AND SCHUSTER and colophon are registered
trademarks of Simon & Schuster Inc.

Designed by Robert Bull Design

Manufactured in the United States of America

1   3   5   7   9   10   8   6   4   2

Library of Congress Cataloging-in-Publication Data is available.

ISBN 0-684-85280-2

The photograph on page 28 is from *French's Index of Differential Diagnosis*
(thirteenth edition), edited by Ian A. D. Bouchier, Harold Ellis,
and Peter R. Fleming, and is reproduced by permission
of Butterworth-Heinemann and the editors.

Acknowledgments

I am grateful to the many physicians who generously shared with me their valuable time and formidable talents despite the fact that 1) there was no fee involved, and 2) they were forewarned that this book was going to be an irresponsible, alarmist work of pseudoliterature that would relentlessly make fun of doctors. In short, these people exhibited either uncommonly bad judgment or uncommonly good nature, or both. Unless otherwise noted, they all practice in the Washington, D.C., area:

Israel Alter; Hal Blumenfeld (New Haven, Conn.); William Bond; Stephen Elgin; Henry Fox; Bruce Kressel; Susan Lacks; Michael D. Levitt (Minneapolis, Minn.); Steven Nadler (Snowmass Village, Colo.); Bruce Orkin; Arnold Ratner; Anthony Reder (Chicago, Ill.); Jonathan Sackier; Marvin Schuster; Alan Singer; Mark Smith; Michael Stanton; Karen Stark (Scottsdale, Ariz.); Robert Stavis (Bryn Mawr, Pa.); Louis Steinberg; Robert Tanenberg; Martin Wolfe; and Lorenz Zimmerman. In particular, I would like to thank Drs. Mitchell Dunn and Louis Y. Korman, who provided invaluable assistance even though, as my personal physicians, they understood better than anyone else the many dark and alarming pathologies of the author. They are terrific doctors, and nice guys. I hereby urge all readers to contract serious, lingering diseases and move to Washington for the honor of being treated by them.

None of these doctors is responsible for any errors of fact contained herein. Any errors of fact contained herein are the fault of, and the sole legal responsibility of, The Error Monster.

I thank my editor at Simon & Schuster, David Rosenthal, who encouraged me to belly up to that thin line dividing the daring from the tasteless, and then gleefully booted my arse right over it. Thanks also to David's assistant, Zoe Wolff, who at twenty-five provides both her boss and me with at least a modicum of maturity and common sense. For his loyalty, enthusiasm, and wisdom I thank my agent, Al Hart, who somehow capably negotiates the complex world of modern publishing while writing all his correspondence on a typewriter. (With carbons.) For their exceptional research assistance, I thank Bobbye Pratt and Michael Farquhar of *The Washington Post*. For their counsel I thank Libby Burger of Glen Mills, Pennsylvania; Joel Achenbach, David Streitfeld, and Frank Ahrens of *The Washington Post*; and Philip Brooker and Tom Shroder of *The Miami Herald*. I am grateful to Donald Graham and Leonard Downie Jr., publisher and executive editor of *The Washington Post*, for permitting one of their editors to write a book like this despite the disrepute it will surely visit upon a great newspaper.

I am particularly indebted to my friend Pat Myers, the World's Funniest Copy Editor, who singlehandedly prevented everyone from discovering what a careless, intellectually shiftless illiterate I am. Pat edited every page of the book, except thsi one.

Finally, I thank my friend Dave Barry, who gave me no assistance whatsoever except in the sense of providing me, through his work, a flawless template for timing, setup, structure, syntax, voice, emphasis, cadence, and word selection, not to mention providing a specific prototype for virtually every joke contained in these pages. I hereby forgive Dave for shamelessly imitating my style all these many years.

To my rib

Contents

Introduction by Dave Barry
15

CHAPTER 1:
Are You a Hypochondriac?
21

CHAPTER 2:
Relax, Hypochondria Never Killed Anyone.
Oh, Wait. Yes, It Did.
31

CHAPTER 3:
The Mind of the Hypochondriac
36

CHAPTER 4:
How Your Doctor Can Kill You
41

CHAPTER 5:
Man. Woman. Birth. Death. Infirmity.
47

CHAPTER 6:
Hypochondria and Me
54

CHAPTER 7:
Hiccups Can Mean Cancer
63

CHAPTER 8:
Headaches: Don't Worry, They're All in Your Head
77

CHAPTER 9:
Interpreting DocSpeak (Hint: "Good" Means "Bad")
83

CHAPTER 10:
Maybe It's Just Nerves (Uh-Oh)
91

CHAPTER 11:
Infarction—Isn't That a Funny Word?
Hahahahaha Thud.
102

CHAPTER 12:
Are You an Alcoholic?
112

CHAPTER 13:
Tumor. Rhymes with "Humor."
116

CHAPTER 14:
Ulcers and Other Visceral Fears
124

CHAPTER 15:
Are You Too Fat? Yes. (I Mean, *Look* at You.)
134

CHAPTER 16:
Snap, Crackle, and Plop (Minor Aches and
Pains That Can Kill You)
138

CHAPTER 17:
Why You Should Not Smoke
147

CHAPTER 18:
Pregnant? That's *Wonderful*! Don't Read This!
149

CHAPTER 19:
Things That Can Take Out an Eye
158

CHAPTER 20:
Oh, Crap (Diagnosis by the Process of Elimination)
170

THE FINAL CHAPTER:
Is Death a Laughing Matter? Of Corpse Not.
181

Bibliography
199

Index
201

Introduction

by Dave Barry

*W**hat kind** of a person is Gene Weingarten? That is not an easy question to answer.

No, wait, I just realized that it's actually a very easy question to answer. Gene Weingarten is a *weird* kind of person.

For example, there was the incident with the tropical fish. This happened back when Gene was my boss at *The Miami Herald*'s Sunday magazine, *Tropic*. We were working on a project called the Tropic Hunt, which was a reader-participation stunt we had dreamed up, in which thousands of our readers would be driving all over south Florida trying to solve a giant, complex puzzle so they could win Valuable Prizes.

To solve one very small part of the hunt, the readers had to count the number of advertisements in *Tropic* for (why not?) fish cemeteries. We created two ads for competing fish cemeteries, one of which boasted that it offered cremation services. To illustrate this feature—bear in mind that this was a very small, inconsequential part of the overall project—Gene spent a day obtaining a rental tuxedo and a tropical fish, and then getting himself professionally photographed as a fish-cemetery funeral director. He was holding a small tropical fish in one hand and—

with a look of sadness and solemn dignity—setting fire to it with a Bic lighter.

Granted, it was a *dead* fish.

But still.

It was during the planning stages for this same hunt that Gene called me up one night and we had this conversation:

> Gene: I ordered fifty thousand candy canes.
> Me: Fifty thousand? Candy canes?

(I should note here that, up to this point in the hunt planning, there had never been any discussion of candy canes.)

> Gene: Yes! But they're *not regular candy canes!*
> Me: They're not?
> Gene: No! They LOOK like regular candy canes, but *they taste orange!*
> Me: They taste orange?
> Gene: Yes! They have an orange taste!
> Me: Huh!
> Gene: So, we can use them to make a *really, really clever puzzle!*
> Me: Huh!
> Gene: Yes!

(Here there was a thoughtful pause.)

> Me: So, how exactly would this puzzle work?
> Gene: I have no idea!

And he didn't, either. But for the next several weeks, he did have fifty thousand red-and-white (but *orange-flavored*) candy canes in his living room, along with several dozen traffic barricades (don't ask). He did, ultimately, find a use for the candy canes.

But still.

Did I mention the time that the group of high-level executives from corporate headquarters came to get a briefing from Gene on his operation? No? OK, here's what happened: A squadron of serious suit-wearing corporate visitors were going around *The*

Miami Herald, getting overviews from the various department heads on the various department operations. When they got to the *Tropic* offices, there was Gene, standing at the conference table, looking the way he usually looks when he is dressed for work, which is the way other men look when they are going to a Halloween party as Harpo Marx.

So Gene, who of course had never read the memo informing him that he was supposed to be giving an overview, started telling the suits about the story he happened to be working on at the moment. This was a cover story *Tropic* was running about a man who tracked hurricanes. To illustrate this story, Gene had a photographer shoot the man hanging from a tree limb, like this:

The gimmick was that the magazine would print the photograph *sideways,* so it would look as though the man's body was being held horizontal by a tremendous wind, like this:

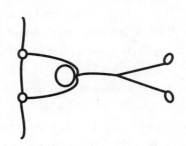

Gene was going to explain this idea to the suits, but it occurred to him that it would be easier just to show them the photograph. So he called over to the art director, Philip Brooker: "Philip, show them the picture of the guy getting blown."

Now, OK, this was an embarrassing mistake, but totally understandable. The suits were pretty cool about it; some of them even chuckled politely. Then they were ready for Gene to continue with his overview.

The problem was, Gene had decided that "Show them the picture of the guy getting blown" was the funniest single line ever delivered in the history of human comedy. He collapsed, facedown, on the conference table, quaking with laughter. The entire room waited patiently for him to finish; finally he pulled himself together and rose back up to face the suits, only to be once again overcome by the life-threatening humor of the situation. And so, back down onto the table he went.

Again, the room waited; again, Gene came back up; again, he went back down, quivering and weeping. The table was now sporting an expanding puddle of drool. Gene went down and came up several more times, like one of those drinking-bird toys. Finally, he came up, and the suits were . . . gone. That was their entire management briefing on the operation of *Tropic* magazine.

Why am I telling you these stories? Because when you read this book, at some point—a fairly early point, I am betting—you're going to say, "What kind of lunatic wrote this?"

The answer, as I hope I've shown, is: A *genuine* lunatic. An *honest* lunatic. Ask the many people who know and love Gene Weingarten if they think he is sane, and they will say, laughingly: "No!" And then, after reflecting for a moment, they will say, seriously: "No."

That's why Gene is the perfect person to write this book. He is not some Johnny-come-lately who is just now adopting hypochondria as a way to sell books. Gene is the most sincere, most dedicated, hardest-working hypochondriac it has ever been my privilege to know. When he tells you all the really awful things that can happen to your body—*that could be happening to your body right now!*—he's not just spewing empty words. He's spewing words about problems that he has spent countless hours convincing himself that he, personally, is suffering from. In the more than fifteen years that I've known him, he, personally, has had more fatal diseases than the entire Indian subcontinent.

I have, on several occasions, turned to Gene for medical advice, and he has never failed to come up with the most depressing possible diagnosis. For example, two years ago I suffered a head injury while playing Lazer Tag with my son. For the next few days, all I wanted to do was sleep. This was starting to make me nervous, so finally I called Gene, who, unlike the so-called "medical profession," is instantly accessible and always willing to take on a new case, no matter how complex, over the phone. I described my symptoms to him, and he said: "I'll get back to you."

He spent several hours doing research—Gene has an extensive medical library—then called me back to let me know that I should get a CAT scan, because I was probably going to die. I'm sure that he suspected this from the first, but he is far too responsible to venture an opinion without knowing the whole story.

As it happened, I did not die. In fact, after talking to Gene, I felt better; I always do. In a way, it's good to know the worst thing that can happen. That's why this book is useful, maybe even therapeutic. Reading it is like going on the Space Mountain ride at Disney World: You experience terror, yes, but when it's over, you're thrilled to still be alive.

Not that you necessarily *will* be.

CHAPTER ONE

Are
You
a Hypochondriac?

***W**e must begin* by abandoning antiquated, stigmatizing notions about the hypochondriac, a person who imagines himself afflicted by disease. Like alcoholism, hypochondria is not the hypochondriac's "fault," or a moral weakness, but a disease.

Hmm.

To hypochondriacs, I offer reassurance: We are no longer living in an era when every little symptom signaled the onset of some dreadful condition with a goofy name, like "consumption" or "whooping cough" or "St. Vitus's dance," disorders that meant you would spend the remainder of your tragically truncated life drooling out your viscera into slop buckets. Today illnesses have really hip names like "astroblastoma," and you drool out your viscera into state-of-the-art, hypoallergenic, FDA-approved polypropylene "viscera receptacles."

Just kidding, hypochondriacs! Good Lord, get a grip. Look out the window. Do you see tumbrels in the streets? Nowadays, nearly everything is curable. Magazines are filled with ads for cancer support groups and "empowerment seminars," with pictures of survivors who are reassuring you that one can go on to have a normal, disease-free life. Typically, these people are wearing wigs that fit like yarmulkes.

Do you suffer from hypochondria? We are all susceptible to it—it is part of our survival instinct, imprinted in our brains from infancy. We are in our crib and our diaper is wet, so we howl and thrash and whimper, and pretty soon someone comes to help us. It is our mom. She coos to us sympathetically and slathers our behind with products that make us smell like the sitting room of a nineteenth-century San Francisco bordello. An important behavioral arc has been established: Complaint brings attention; attention brings relief.

(The more loving and attentive your mom is, the more likely you are to become a hypochondriac. This is simple anthropology. Remember Binti the gorilla, the ape whose maternal instincts were so strong she rescued an injured child? It is a little-known fact that Binti's children are sniveling pantywaists. While the other young zoo gorillas are engaged in ordinary gorilla activities such as pleasuring themselves in front of kindergarten classes and consuming one another's lice, Binti's kids are off in a corner, fretfully examining their armpits for lumps.)

As he leaves infancy, of course, the developing hypochondriac must refine the nature of his tantrums. Adults cannot continue to demand attention by fussing and mewling and smearing their excreta everywhere, unless they are professional athletes. And so the hypochondriac learns the art of suffering in silence—courageous silence, deafening silence, valiant, stolid, stoic, selfless, resolute, gloomy, lip-trembling silence, until you have to strangle him to death with the drawstring of his bathrobe.

It is easy to make fun of hypochondriacs. The hypochondriac is at war with his own body. The ordinary person will notice a slight spastic tugging on his eyelid, that rhythmic twitching we all feel from time to time, and go, "Hmm."

That doesn't happen with the hypochondriac. A hypochondriac would not go "Hmm" unless you told him there was a new fatal disease whose first symptom is the inability to say "Hmm." Then he would say "Hmm" 1,723 times a day until he got laryngitis and could no longer say "Hmm," which would of course constitute proof he is dying.

No, if a hypochondriac gets an eyelid tic, his mind will instantly race through everything he knows about twitching—health textbooks he has read and articles he has downloaded from arcane medical databases—and he will eventually focus on the most frightening evidence he can think of, no matter how dubious its authority, such as the scene in the movie *Airplane!* in which Leslie Nielsen, playing a doctor, describes the symptoms of fatal food poisoning, which begins with twitching, and the pilot, played by Peter Graves, dies farting.

So the hypochondriac will *know* he has been poisoned. He will call the Poison Control Center.

> Hypochondriac: My eyelid is twitching once every six point four seconds.
>
> Poison Control Person: *(Pause)* Omigod.
>
> Hypochondriac: OMIGOD? *(Beatbeatbeatbeatbeatbeatbeat)*
>
> Poison Control Person: Quick. You need to prepare an antidote. Do you have any anchovies?
>
> Hypochondriac: Yes!
>
> Poison Control Person: OK, now do exactly what I say. Make a drink of mashed anchovies, root beer, and tartar-control toothpaste . . .

My point is that Poison Control people are shitheads. They love to have their little fun with hypochondriacs. The whole *world* loves to have its fun with hypochondriacs, and I am frankly tired of it.

Listen, hypochondriacs. This book will not insult your intelligence by telling you to grow up, that it's all in your mind. It will insult your intelligence in far more sophisticated ways. This book is going to feed your disease, symptom by symptom, chapter by chapter, until—to use complicated medical terminology—you are so gorged on your own self-pity you puke it all out. And as everyone knows, puking it all out is a great way to purge the body of toxins. Unless it leads to a rupture of the esophagus, septicemia, peritonitis, febrile dementia, and death.

This book will also describe many rudimentary medical tests that, in the hands of the trained clinician, can be invaluable diagnostic tools. These tests are so simple that you could perform them on yourself, in the privacy of your home. Not that you should. Doctors have spent years studying the proper techniques of physical examination. No reputable writer would encourage untrained persons to engage in self-diagnosis, particularly hypochondriacs, who may be needlessly alarmed. For quick reference I will thumbnail each test with a handy icon.

Quick! Go to the mirror. Open your mouth. Look at your uvula, the thing that hangs down at the back like a garden slug. Is it pulsing? It shouldn't be. When your uvula throbs in time with your heartbeat it is called Mueller's sign, and it can indicate heart disease! You could die!

Now insert the tips of your three middle fingers into your mouth, making a vertical stack, without touching your lips or teeth. If you cannot open your mouth that wide, you might have temporomandibular joint syndrome; worse, you might have systemic sclerosis, a grotesque progressive illness in which your skin hardens and contracts and can slowly garrote the life out of you.

With your palm facing you, tap lightly on the very center of your wrist. You are performing the Tinel test. If you feel a radiating numbness in your hand, you might have early carpal tunnel syndrome, which can eventually turn your hands into appendages as useful and attractive as a tyrannosaurus's.

In the end this book is going to present a surefire cure for hypochondria—a dramatic, natural remedy as effective as Bactine on a boo-boo. I could disclose it here, but I won't. This is a literary technique called foreshadowing, previously employed by famous literary individuals such as William Shakespeare. In the hands of the unscrupulous, foreshadowing can be nothing more than misleading hype. The responsible writer promises no more than he can deliver. I will say only this: I am going to keep hinting at my cure for hypochondria until I finally disclose it, and you will have an orgasm.

To find out if this book is "for you," take this simple Grade-Ur-Self Multiple-Choice Test. There are nine questions. Score one point for each answer numbered 1, two points for each answer numbered 2, and three points for each answer numbered 3.

THE HYPOCHONDRIA SELF-EXAM

A. Carefully wash and dry your hands. Now touch your left nipple with your right hand. Knead the nipple between your thumb and forefinger, rolling it gently but firmly in a counterclockwise direction. What do you feel?

　1. Stupid.

　2. A nipple.

　3. Small, benign enlargements and/or impacted pores that are probably no cause for alarm.

B. You feel you might have a fever. So you:

　1. Crank up the air-conditioning.

　2. Take your temperature.

　3. Take your temperature, and when you insert the thermometer you are pretty sure you notice an extra lump in that thing under the tongue that looks like a sea urchin, so you walk around with your tongue in the air, asking everyone if they see anything wrong, only they can't understand you because it comes out "Arll Iralll lallrhal?"

C. Within 38 to 40 minutes of eating a heavy meal, do you sometimes find that your pyloric sphincter fails to relax adequately, causing excessive peptic digestion accompanied by mild-to-moderate upper gastric distress and followed 18 to 22 hours later by chalky stools?

　1. Huh?

　2. Sphincter? Wha?

　3. Yes.

D. When did you last see a doctor?

　1. Two years ago or more.

　2. In the past two years.

3. You are reading this in your doctor's office. You are having him check out that left nipple, just to be sure.

E. You notice a slight pain in your armpit when you lift your arm in a certain way. Do you:

1. Stop lifting your arm in that certain way.
2. Check for lumps.
3. Check for lumps. Finding none, check for nodes or lesions or garfunkels. Finding none, get a brain scan. Finding no abnormalities, you contrive to have a conversation with a trusted friend wherein you casually mention that you know of a person who noticed a slight pain in his armpit when he lifted his arm a certain way, and your friend says yes, she once knew someone like that who later developed dysentery and pooped himself to death, and suddenly you have to go to the bathroom real bad.

F. Do you have any moles?

1. I don't know.
2. Yes. Maybe I should get them looked at.
3. Yes, but they have not changed appreciably in the last 18 months. I have Polaroids.

G. Systemic lupus erythematosus is a serious, debilitating, potentially fatal autoimmune disease involving periodic, episodic occurrences of some or all of the following symptoms: fatigue, muscle aches, rashes, nausea, dry mouth, chest pain, headaches, bruising of the skin, tenderness in the joints, forgetfulness. Do you think you might have systemic lupus erythematosus?

1. Nah.
2. Why? What have you heard?
3. If it were only that simple.

H. Would you marry a proctologist?

1. No.
2. No, unless I loved the person very, very much.
3. No, unless I had polyps.

I. How do you think you will die?

1. In bed, surrounded by weeping children and grandchildren.
2. Flying through the windshield of your car.
3. Flying through the windshield of your car after suffering a "cerebrovascular accident," or stroke, probably linked to undiagnosed atherosclerosis, thrombotic endocarditis, or hemorrhagic telangiectasia.

GRADING

Score of 9–10: You should buy this book because you are entirely too cavalier about your body. Vigilance is critical to good health.

Score of 11–19: You should buy this book to feel superior to the people in the next group. A positive mental attitude is critical to good health.

Score of 20–27: You are a hypochondriac. If you do not buy this book, you will die.

Score of 28 or higher: You are an imbecile. You have already bought this book and plan to use it as your family's primary medical text.

There are other excellent books available to those persons concerned with their health. In the interests of fairness and full disclosure, I will briefly describe these volumes and list their principal advantages and disadvantages.

The first group consists of books with names like *The Family Medical Guide,* or *The Home Medical Encyclopedia,* or *The Doctors' Guide to Good Health,* generally published by the American Medical Association or other renowned physicians' organizations. These are helpful, responsible diagnostic books, featuring listings of symptoms in easy-to-follow flow charts, each chart terminating in a row of exclamation points urging you to see your physician without delay.

The second group are clinical texts, intended for doctors and available mostly in medical bookstores and libraries, containing lines like this, from page 458 of *Current Medical Diagnosis and Treatment, 1995:* "Disorders such as disseminated intravascular coagulation, thrombotic thrombocytopenic purpura, hemolytic-uremic syndrome, hypersplenism, and sepsis are easily excluded by the absence of system illness. Thus, patients with isolated thrombocytopenia with no other abnormal findings almost certainly have immune thrombocytopenia."

These books are characterized by the use of humongously scientific Latin-influenced terms such as "sternutation"[1] and "epistaxis"[2] and "cutis anserina"[3] and "pyrexia"[4] and "diaphoresis"[5] and "singultus,"[6] which are too important and complicated to be understood by unschooled morons such as yourself.

Many of these medical books also contain pages of photographs, such as this one, reprinted from *French's Differential Diagnosis* (1979):

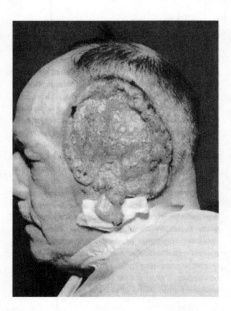

---

1. Sneezing.
2. Nosebleed.
3. Goose bumps.
4. Fever.
5. Sweating.
6. Hiccups.

So these books can be highly entertaining, though they cost much more than my book and make you vomit.

The third type consists of books arranged on endless shelves labeled "alternative medicine." These usually begin with solemn advice against succumbing to quackery, followed by a simple nine-step formula for curing lymphomas via the teachings of Mohammed Ibn Rajneesh and the use of beet suppositories. Alternative medicine books take elaborate measures to appear serious and scientific. I am right now leafing through *Alternatives in Cancer Therapy,* by Ross Pelton and Lee Overholser, featuring an endorsement on the cover by Linus Pauling, the two-time Nobel laureate. *Alternatives in Cancer Therapy* soberly evaluates treatments that include eating mistletoe, taking enemas made from strong coffee, and drinking urine.

My book is like none of those.[7] Unlike the family medical guides, this book will dispense no practical medical advice whatsoever. Unlike the alternative medical books, it will advance no mountebank cures. Unlike the medical texts, it will not be condescending to the reader.[8] It will mention thrombotic thrombocytopenic purpura only for the purpose of observing that, among all diseases the author has encountered in the course of his extensive medical research requiring many, many footnotes,[9] it has the second-funniest name.[10]

Last, let me say that although this book will raise some legitimate concerns about health, it will not use scare tactics to inflame the public's fears in the manner that, say, untreated

---

7. It is also unlike *Hystories,* a popular 1997 book by Elaine Showalter suggesting that many trendy diseases of the modern era—such as chronic fatigue syndrome— are not real, but hysterical reactions to the tensions of modern life. This book led to strong opposition by CFS sufferers, who claimed it belittled them and their affliction. Their opposition dramatically increased sales of *Hystories,* an obscure scholarly treatise, because chronic fatigue syndrome sufferers kept showing up to picket Ms. Showalter's public appearances. I wonder if they wore bunny rabbit slippers and Dr. Denton's pajamas, with the little tushy flap in the back. I hereby express my solidarity with CFS sufferers and other whining nutcakes, including victims of "seasonal affective disorder." I will fight to the death for their right to picket my book.

8. "Condescending" is a great big word that means "talking down to."

9. Some of my footnotes even have footnotes.[11]

10. The funniest name: "beer potomania." See Chapter 12, "Are You an Alcoholic?"

11. Like this one.

appendicitis can inflame the appendix until it bursts, choking the bloodstream with deadly toxins and snuffing out your life in fifteen minutes of writhing agony. We are living in an era of fabulous preventive medicine. After all, it is not every day that some guy goes to the doctor because he is peeing a lot and learns he has a prostate the size of a bagpipe, though I personally know of two people this happened to.

They did not buy this book either, and now they are dead.

CHAPTER TWO

Relax, Hypochondria
Never Killed Anyone.
Oh, Wait. Yes, It Did.

---

eople have always been worried about their health, and
some people have always been more worried than others.
The ancient Greeks coined the term *hypochondrion* to indicate
the part of the torso beneath the rib cage, which is where most
early hypochondriacs imagined their pains. Typically, the sufferer never got better, attributing his condition to what the ancient Greek doctors considered fanciful, even laughable causes.
Think about that. These were primitive times. If you had a *real*
case of, say, influenza, the finest medical minds in the world
would consult on your case and decide you had an evil salaman-
der dwelling in your spleen. What could the hypochondriac possibly have imagined that seemed bizarre to these people?

> First Greek Doctor: I'm at my wits' end with Eucalyptus. He blames his
> sore throat on—get this—teensy invisible creatures that entered his
> body through the nose when someone *else* sneezed!
> Second Greek Doctor: Har har har. What a bozo. But he does seem to be
> ill. Just to be safe, I would follow established medical procedure.
> First Greek Doctor: Agreed. We shall flay him with the tailbone of an ass.

Thousands of years later, hypochondria still poses a diagnostic dilemma for the medical practitioner. On the one hand, taking seriously the brooding of an obvious hypochondriac compromises the noblest tenets of medicine and, by giving credence to his complaints, may even aggravate the poor wretch's condition. On the other hand, the poor wretch is a potential source of tens of thousands of dollars in fees over many, many years.

Faced with this dilemma, most doctors have adopted the following checklist for evaluating a suspected hypochondriac and deciding whether to treat him:

1. Does this person have medical insurance?
2.

The fact is, attention from a doctor may make a hypochondriac feel better, but it won't cure him. Over the years, well-intentioned physicians have tried everything, to no avail.

In his 1961 book, *Minds That Came Back,* Dr. W. C. Alvarez reports on the case of a man who was convinced he had a frog in his stomach: "We gave him an emetic, and while he was vomiting, we slipped a frog into the basin. The man was thrilled; he felt so justified, and he was grateful. The only trouble was that he returned the next day to tell us we had been a bit too late—a dozen baby frogs had hatched out and were hopping about in his stomach."

Many famous people were hypochondriacs: Molière, Voltaire, Jonathan Swift, Rudyard Kipling, Ludwig van Beethoven, Immanuel Kant, Robert Burns, Jesus Christ.[1] Enrico Caruso used a dentist's mirror to examine his vocal cords every day, convinced against all medical evidence that he was subject to alarming growths and swellings. John Adams, our second president, predicted his own death at thirty-five, and then again at forty, because he felt himself afflicted by ill humors. He somehow survived his fifties convinced he could not possibly make it into

---

1. I made this last one up. That is why it is important to read footnotes.

his sixties, so infirm was he. He lived through his seventies with the chill of death's gnarled hand upon his rheumy shoulder. He spent his eighties with one foot in the grave and the other in a pot of Epsom salts. At last, his fears proved sound. Adams died midway through his ninety-first year and remains the oldest ex-president ever.

During a journey in which he shared a coach compartment with a woman with swollen legs, the poet Percy Bysshe Shelley[2] imagined he had caught elephantiasis. For months afterward, he would examine himself for signs of the illness, which causes grotesque enlargement of the legs and, in men, the scrotum. He policed his acquaintances scrupulously to make certain no one could possibly transmit the illness to him. Shelley's biographer Thomas Hogg reports this singular event:

> When many young ladies were standing up for a country dance, he caused wonderful consternation among these charming creatures by walking slowly along the row of girls and curiously surveying them, placing his eyes close to their necks and bosoms, and feeling their breasts and bare arms, in order to ascertain whether any of the fair ones had taken the horrible disease. He proceeded with so much gravity and seriousness, and his looks were so woebegone, that they did not resist, or resent, the extraordinary liberties.

James Boswell, the eighteenth-century Scottish essayist and biographer, would lie in bed at night unable to sleep, convinced his testicles were swelling. Once, he ordered a doctor to bleed him to relieve him of the poisons he felt were making him ill and causing him nightmares. He confessed he enjoyed watching public hangings because it distracted him from the fear of contracting venereal disease.

Hypochondria afflicts the famous and the obscure alike, though most of our best anecdotal evidence concerns celebrities.

---

2. What kind of a name is Bysshe? What is *that* all about? Most people with idiotic middle names simply don't use them. How many of us, for example, know that Abraham Lincoln's middle name was Thptsk?

That is because there is no shortage of jealous, petty ingrates hanging around famous people, willing to betray their privacy for a couple of bucks or a cheap laugh. There are name-droppers everywhere.

This reminds me of the day I personally drove Dick Cavett and his producer to an event in the South Bronx. It was 1972. I was twenty-one. Dick sat in the backseat of my car. His producer sat next to me. Doggedly, I tried to engage the famed talk-show host in conversation. I asked him something suitably sophisticated, such as, "So, Mr. Cavett, what do you think about the state of stand-up comedy in America?" and he answered, "Mrphrprm." This surprised me because Dick Cavett's diction is ordinarily quite elegant, as anyone knows who has ever heard those old ads for Hormel meat products, in which he makes processed hog snouts sound like *boeuf bourguignon*.

I tried again with a less boring question. Something about underpants.

"Mrphrc," he said.

Finally, I looked in the rearview mirror. Dick Cavett, the master TV interviewer, was talking with a handkerchief clapped over his nose and mouth. He looked like an actor endlessly rehearsing his great vomit scene.

"Dick is a little concerned about catching cold," the producer informed me with the determinedly cheerful expression of a mom assuring a neighbor that little Jason's consumption of sidewalk pigeon shit is perfectly normal.

In terms of risk taking, however, Dick Cavett is a bomb-squad demolition expert compared with Marcel Proust.[3] The nihilistic French novelist was so afraid of catching cold that he became a lifelong recluse, spending all his time in a bedroom with walls lined in cork to muffle the insalubrious sounds of civilization. When called upon to serve as best man at his brother's wedding, Proust forced himself to go, but only after fortifying himself with three overcoats and several mufflers, and padding his chest and

---

3. This is, to my knowledge, the first time Dick Cavett and Marcel Proust have appeared together in the same sentence.

collar with layers of cotton. He was so immobilized that he could not sit down and had to stand in the aisle during the service.

The Greatest Hypochondriac of All Time, however, was the American poet Sara Teasdale.

Sara was a woman of heroic gloom.
Anguish oozed from her tortured womb.
O Stygian depths, O life, you accursed vip'rous crutch!
(That's what all her poems sound like, pretty much.)

Sara was a lifelong melancholic. She felt she had "weak veins" and particularly feared a stroke. Once, in 1928, after a particularly bouncy cab ride in Central Park, she became certain she must have suffered a life-threatening blood clot, or possibly a spinal injury. Her back and neck ached. At her insistence, she was hospitalized, but X-rays revealed no fractures. Masseuses, osteopaths, and neurologists were summoned. "I know what blows on the head mean," Sara wrote to a friend. "Rheumatism often develops from an injury of this sort, and it seems to have attacked me practically all over." She hired a nurse for round-the-clock care.

But that was only a preamble. Sara Teasdale entered the Hypochondria Hall of Fame one day in 1933 when a small blood vessel burst in her hand, creating a purpled, spidery bruise.

Sara panicked. She decided this was the first sign of the massive embolism she had been expecting all her life. She knew all about what a stroke could do. She had researched it ceaselessly. She was not about to endure the indignity of it, or subject her loved ones to a lifetime of caring for a dull-eyed vegetable. And so she grimly took to her bath.

That is where her nurse found her the next day. The coroner concluded that her health had been fine, apart from the massive dose of sleeping pills that had killed her—and a small, harmless black-and-blue mark on her hand.

So there you have it, hypochondriacs.

Not only is your disease chronic, it can be fatal.

You're welcome.

CHAPTER THREE

The Mind
of
the Hypochondriac

The hypochondriac stands up one day and feels a little dizzy. This is an ordinary sensation; it happens to all of us, a mild circulatory disturbance. But the hypochondriac is now instantly alert. He can't recall ever noticing this before. He is no expert, but it seems to have multiple implications. Logic tells him it might involve the heart, the lungs, or even the brain.

But he does not panic. The hypochondriac knows he is a hypochondriac. In a sense, this is his greatest comfort. Behind the certitude that he is deathly ill is a sneaking suspicion that it is all in his head. So he just tucks this moment into the back of his mind. Alas, that is the part of the brain that most bedevils the hypochondriac. It is where the mischief is born.

He starts casually monitoring himself. Testing. Lying on his back and then suddenly bounding to his feet, like a Whack-a-Mole. There is the dizziness again! Maybe he looks dizziness up in a home medical guide. He has sixteen of them.

Under "dizziness" there are many subheadings.

Subheading: ". . . in heart disease."

Subheading: ". . . in cerebral arteriopathy."

Subheading: ". . . in polycythemia rubra vera."

The list is as long as a mortician's face.

The hypochondriac cannot help but notice the entry right after "dizziness"—"dyspnea," which *also* has ". . . in heart disease" under it.

Just out of curiosity, he flips to the section on "dyspnea" and it turns out to mean "breathlessness."

There is no immediate connection between these two conditions beyond the accident of their proximity on the page, but this is of no consequence to the hypochondriac. See, he *has* noticed dyspnea. He seems to get out of breath more easily of late. All other possible causes—aging, smoking, a sedentary lifestyle—do not at this moment occur to him. So he begins to watch himself, to *notice* things. He will climb a hill he goes up every day and realize he is somewhat out of breath. Has he felt this way before? The next time, he will follow a young woman up the hill, matching her step for step, and then, at the top, he will compare his breathing rate to hers. This will require him to carefully observe the heaving of her chest. But for some reason, she keeps walking away from him.

Does he smell bad? Is he perspiring excessively?

Why, yes, he is! His hands feel clammy, suddenly.

Back to the books. He looks up sweating. It can be a symptom of leukemia and encephalitis and a whole bunch of things he has never heard of: pyonephrosis, acromegaly, Graves's disease, hypoglycemia. Now he is nearly insane with worry. He goes to a doctor. The doctor listens to his heart, takes his blood pressure, and pronounces him fine!

And he *is* fine. Now he feels great! As he is leaving the doctor's office, though, he will notice a slight stitch in his side . . .

The fact is, most people are concerned about their health. But when does that concern cross the line from prudence to obsession? What is it that distinguishes the ordinary person from the hypochondriac?

In less enlightened times, the answer seemed easy. Hypochondriacs were thought of as whining, self-absorbed cowards. In the popular conception, they waddled around in bathrobes with ice packs on their heads and thermometers in their mouths. Doctors treated them as though they were feebleminded.

This should not be surprising. Through history, medicine has always been guilty of perpetrating hurtful, inaccurate stereotypes. For example, medical science used to categorize homosexuality as a psychiatric disorder caused by domineering mothers; its so-called "symptoms" were preening, mincing, flouncing, bitching, consumption of Midori watermelon liqueur, etc. Nowadays we recognize that homosexuality is a normal condition, caused by failed liberal social policies.

Similarly, we now know that hypochondria afflicts all types of people. And though we still do not know its causes or its cure, we have come a long way toward defining just who the hypochondriac is. There are no reliable clinical tests for hypochondria, but some emergency room doctors have devised their own screening procedure, known, delicately, as "a positive review of symptoms." The hypochondriac will tend to answer yes to any question, so long as it is delivered with appropriate gravity. The two best-known screening tests: "Does your stool glow in the dark?" and "Do your teeth itch?"[1] Dr. Martin Wolfe, a Washington, D.C., specialist in parasitic diseases, deals occasionally with people who complain of bugs crawling out of their skin. Sometimes, bugs *do* crawl out of the skin, of course. Dr. Wolfe's screening question: "Did it have a mustache?"

The hypochondriac does not "imagine" pain, the way the ordinary person might fantasize, say, about blasting the homer that wins the World Series or getting that job she always dreamed about, or writing a fraudulent medical book that becomes a runaway best-seller, making him so wealthy he never has to work again and can buy sport utility vehicles and throw them away after using them once, like disposable razors. No, the hypochondriac actually *feels* his pain. The mechanics of how this happens remain a mystery, but the fact that it happens is indisputable.

This is not as peculiar as it seems. The human brain is an

---

1. Emergency rooms can be a crucible for hypochondria, and a carnival of misunderstandings. People who use emergency rooms for primary medical care tend not to be the most knowledgeable patients. In medical schools, emergency room stories are legion. One woman is said to have informed an admitting doctor her baby was having a relapse of "the smilin' mighty Jesus." Eventually, he figured it out: spinal meningitis. A Washington-area emergency medical technician reports that a patient told him *her* baby was on regular dosage of "peanut butter balls"—phenobarbital.

amazing organ capable of astonishing feats. Doctors have long noted the existence of a phenomenon known as the "placebo effect": When illnesses of all types are treated with sugar pills, and the patients are told they are getting medicine, as many as 35 percent get cured anyway. The implications of this are astounding. It means that either

1. Sugar is a tragically underutilized medical resource; *or,*
2. Doctors are swine. Because what about the 65 percent of patients who *don't* get cured?

Imagine the scene in the consulting room: "Well, Mr. Farquhar, I have good news and bad news. The bad news is that the canker sore on your lip didn't respond to medication and has migrated to your groin, where it has progressed to a particularly nasty case of thrombotic thrombocytopenic purpura. The good news is, the medication you didn't respond to was . . . a Domino demi-lump! Ha ha ha h— (*Sound of stethoscope inserted into nostril.*)"

The point is, if the brain can relieve pain, surely it can create it.

My own extensive research into hypochondria suggests that the hypochondriac fits a basic personality pattern that might best be illustrated through the use of a Venn diagram, an extremely scientific visual aid utilized, for some reason, in the sixth grade and never again. Venn diagrams examine the relationships between groups of people via simple geometric comparisons.

For example, Fig. 1 represents a general population breakdown.

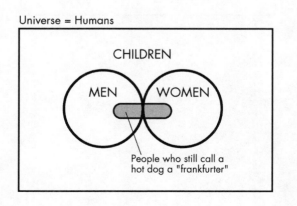

Fig. 1

Get the idea? OK, now let's look at hypochondriacs (Fig. 2).

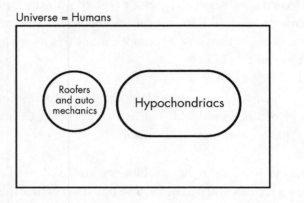

Fig. 2

This is a helpful, but still inadequate, profile. Fig. 3 completes the picture.

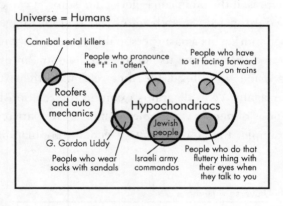

Fig. 3

CHAPTER FOUR

How Your
Doctor Can
Kill You

A doctor's reputation is made by the number of eminent men who die under his care.

—GEORGE BERNARD SHAW

A number of doctors have studied hypochondria, but very few openly specialize in its treatment. The only one I could find through a global search of the Internet was a Dr. Ingvard Wilhelmsen in Bergen, Norway. Norwegians are apparently prone to hypochondria because Norway has a high standard of living, meaning that people have a great deal of leisure time in which to contemplate their lives, which are spent in a dank, hellish place that could depress a hyena. Norwegians have it so bad that when they flee Norway in search of a more hospitable clime, they often head for North Dakota.

In my relentless search for information, as a service to hypochondriacs, I telephoned Norway. I had many questions. I wished to pool my commonsense knowledge of the subject with Dr. Wilhelmsen's professional expertise. Together, I hoped, we could bring a measure of solace to persons afflicted by this much maligned condition. This was my conversation, as reflected by my notes:

Me: Is Dr. Wilhelmsen in?

Norwegian Person: *Va? Schlift wann kumm?*

Me: Er, is the doctor in? DO YOU SPEAK ENGLISH?

Norwegian Person: *Schmu? Isfaehrkt?*

Me: OK, sorry. Never mind.

So, big shot Wilhelmsen proved no help at all.

This should not come as a surprise. Doctors are not always the most helpful people. The vaunted Hippocratic oath[1] requires doctors to do no harm, but medical texts are full of warnings about procedures that often go seriously awry. Some are minor. Some are not. For example, doctors treating you for hypernatremia, a serious electrolyte imbalance caused by dehydration, will sometimes accidentally overdose you on water and potassium. This creates a brain condition called central pontine myelinolysis, leaving you a quadriplegic, or a corpse.

Some years ago my father went to see a doctor for a routine physical exam. My father is a gentle, self-effacing man who does not wish to make a fuss or be a bother to others. He is the sort of man who, in a restaurant, will not ask for a translation prior to ordering a dish with a fancy French name. Then, rather than complain, he will consume it even though it appears to be rat fetuses in béchamel sauce.

A few hours after his medical exam, my father phoned me and reported that everything went well, and were the kids home from school yet, and he is dying. Now, my father is pretty old and his hearing isn't what it used to be.[2] I figured he had misheard the doctor. So I called the doctor.

The doctor gave me good news and bad news. The good news was that there was apparently nothing additionally wrong with

---

1. Have you ever read the vaunted Hippocratic oath? It is loony. It begins by swearing allegiance to "all the gods and goddesses." Then it promises to revere the person who taught you medicine and support him financially. Then it says abortion sucks. Only then does it get down to business, saying you should not be greedy, should cause no injury, should respect your patient's privacy, and should not sleep with her.

2. Actually, his hearing was never much to begin with; when I was a lad, I would frequently make some innocuous statement at the dinner table—say, "I got a B on my final"—and find out weeks later that my father believed I'd said I had gotten beer on my vagina, but was too polite to inquire further.

my father's hearing. The bad news was that my father had a heart condition so severe it was a wonder he was still walking around, of apparently sound mind, and unaware of his predicament. The doctor said my father would progress rapidly into a nearly catatonic state in which he would need round-the-clock nursing care, his mind slowly deteriorating into an unpredictable form of dementia typically leading to slack-jawed insensibility and, inevitably, death, which would come as a mercy.

That was six years ago. My father has since celebrated his eighty-fourth birthday. He has won a national math-puzzle competition. He still does my taxes. He regularly beats me at poker, though he seems to lose fairly consistently to his grandchildren. He baby-sits for my dogs. I go to his place to watch football games because he lets me smoke cigars and swear. There is nothing wrong with his heart. Never was.

I do not mean to cast aspersions on the entire medical profession because of one bonehead's mistake. The medical profession is and has always been peopled by caring professionals operating at the very pinnacle of human achievement, though it does give one pause that the official cause of death of Warren Harding, soberly pronounced by the finest attending physicians of the day, was "a fit of apoplexy."

My point is that doctors tend to be profoundly sure of themselves, even when they have no idea what they are talking about.[3]

I used to blame the arrogance of medicine on modernity, on the technologies that have elevated the physician to the role of divine mechanic: Mr. Godwrench. In my thinking, doctors of earlier, simpler times were probably just fellas, humble dis-

---

3. Medical quackery has a long and storied history. When King Charles II of England suffered a minor stroke in 1685, the finest medical minds of the time were summoned to the royal bedchambers. First, to rid the king's body of all poisons, they drained him of a quart of blood. Then they further desiccated him with emetics and enemas. Over the next few days they shaved the king's scalp and singed it with hot irons. They crammed sneezing powder in his nose and let him blast out his few remaining drops of liquid. They slathered his body with sticky hot plasters, and then, when they hardened, ripped them off; by this time, Charles was doubtless too weak to scream. The monarch was sinking rapidly. But the doctors were on top of it. They were giants of their profession. They drilled holes in his head, to drain off the bad humors and a few more pints of blood. Alas, it was no use. Five days after the treatment began, the king breathed his last, effusively thanking his physicians for their heroic efforts to save him.

pensers of commonsense therapeutics, only a dram more sophisticated than the medieval barber-surgeon, painfully aware of the limitations of their science and of themselves.

That is what I thought until, recently, I happened upon a book published in 1902. *The Cottage Physician,* written by a consortium of "the best physicians and surgeons of modern practice," was a popular home medical text offering sage advice on the prevention and treatment of disease. The most striking thing about this book is the authority with which it presumes to speak on medical matters large and small. Cautioning against placing yourself in the hands of charlatans, it promises "The Very Best and Most Approved Remedies and Methods of Treatment Known to Advanced Practitioners."

To wit:

The diabetes sufferer is informed that his condition is of his own making, caused by excessive sexual intercourse, by generally intemperate living, and by "copious evacuation of the bowels." For treatment, the licentious, poop-crazy scoundrel is advised to wear flannel clothing, to eat no vegetables, to vomit frequently, and to take suppositories carved from bars of soap.

A man's hair loss may be arrested through the application of a pomade of lard and rum.

Difficulty in urinating requires a marshmallow enema.

Women, the book informs us, are mysterious creatures, so constitutionally inferior that they must be coddled throughout life. Fortunately, aside from pregnancy—a time when the practitioner must deal with a woman's inexplicable, insatiable appetites for nonfoodstuffs such as clay, chalk, and charcoal—women's medical problems are fairly simple, and easy to diagnose and treat. Almost everything that befalls them occurs because of their womb. Sometimes the womb "falls." Sometimes it swells. Women are particularly susceptible to hysteria; it is caused by the womb. Doctors recommend that the victim of hysteria be treated in the following manner: Her hands should be bound to prevent her from injuring herself. A piece of steel, heated in boiling water for two minutes and wrapped in silk, should be passed down her spine. And last, an enema should be administered consisting of turpentine and stinkweed. During this procedure, it is essential that the woman be kept "tranquil."

Tranquillity is also prescribed at other critical times, for men and women alike. "If within an hour or two of any violent mental emotion the impregnating act follows," the book cautions, "the offspring has that predominating trait throughout life." The doctor-authors theorize that this explains how the villainous Aaron Burr could have been born to two parents of irreproachable character. At the instant of conception, they suggest, Mr. and/or Mrs. Burr must have somehow permitted their piety to slip, and entertained an impure thought.

Flipping through this wonderful book, one discovers that almost every ailment—rheumatism, cataracts, eczema, convulsions, sciatica—responds well to generous and sustained doses of laxatives. Cancerous tumors—thankfully confined mostly to persons of "scrofulous constitutions"—may be reliably eliminated by application of a poultice of warm milk and figs.

Proper nutrition is essential to good health; one must consume not only the egg but also the shell. Tetanus is cured by "pouring cold water on the head from a considerable height" and by turpentine enemas.

The discovery of this book set me on a journey to find others. It turns out almost every used-book store has one or two of them, and though they differ in content and philosophy, they are similar in the impressive medical pedigrees of their authors and in the certitude with which they deliver remedies. One of these, the *Obstetrical Journal of Great Britain and Ireland* (1873), reports favorable results from the treatment of constipation with arsenic.

The *Text-Book of the Principles and Practices of Nursing* (third edition, 1938) prescribes, for the treatment of a persistent cough, heroin. *Lessons in Physiology and Hygiene*, a medical text published in 1895, observes that the size of one's brain is directly proportional to one's intelligence and then dryly notes, without further comment, that women have smaller brains than men.

In the 1875 *Nashville Journal of Medicine*, a Dr. Bowling advises that persons permanently refrain from eating any fruits or vegetables. They can be deadly, he says, citing several rather thin case studies, including this one: "One of the most beautiful and accomplished young ladies in the city ate two or three pickles, and died."

It was after reading some of these books that I entered the hospital for some minor outpatient surgery. There, I entrusted myself to an excellent doctor of my acquaintance, one of the very best physicians and surgeons of modern practice. He gave me a marshmallow enema.

Just kidding! That would have been ridiculous! We have come a long way since then. No, the doctor stabbed me in the side with a gigantic needle and yanked out a little plug of flesh, just to see what it was made of.

I was not at all concerned.

Why should I be?

He assured me this was One of the Most Approved Remedies and Methods of Treatment Known to Advanced Practitioners.

I am certain that a hundred years from now, it will not look at all foolish.

CHAPTER FIVE

Man. Woman.
Birth. Death.
Infirmity.

You would think that as medicine has become more sophisticated, the incidence of hypochondria would diminish. It hasn't. By all accounts, it is increasing.

There are three reasons. The first is medical insurance. To understand the insidious impact of medical insurance on hypochondria, it would be helpful to imagine life before medical insurance. Imagine you were a Jewish peasant in Russia in 1903. If you felt sick, you trudged twelve miles to the doctor. His fee would be a goat. Which means not only did you have to walk the twelve miles from your shtetl to his shtetl, but you had to schlep the goat. On the way, Cossacks on horseback would harass you and make fun of your beard, and they might even take your goat.

Everything about this system discouraged hypochondria. You would do your best to convince yourself that your symptoms, whatever they were, were negligible and that medical attention was unnecessary. Or you attempted to treat yourself. You would try some random nostrum, say, taking a sitz bath in molasses and chicken hearts. And because most ailments eventually resolve themselves anyway, your symptoms would eventually disappear and you would conclude that whatever you did had worked.[1] All over Russia, people would be curing themselves by drinking monkey urine or yodeling with beetles in their mouths. Yes, they were nincompoops, but they were not hypochondriacs. Behind the whole system was the fact that getting medical attention was difficult and costly. Now your doctor is a few minutes away. Your only fee is a $5 "copayment," which is so puny doctors don't even keep it; it goes into a plastic cup near the reception desk, for gum and panty hose.

The second reason hypochondria is on the rise is the proliferation of scientific studies. It used to be that major achievements in medicine were made by solitary eccentrics like Louis Pasteur, puttering around in their basement laboratories, discovering that bread mold could cure syphilis. Their medical tools were a ball peen hammer, six worms, and spit. These days, things are much more complicated. Scientists work in teams, sponsored by universities, funded by gigantic grants. In order to justify their time and keep their sponsors happy, they must periodically issue reports, however obvious their conclusions may be. A study I just read actually concluded that small thin women tend to live longer than big fat women. (Next: BAD TO BE EATEN BY WILD DOGS, EXPERTS SAY.)

The official house organ of study-promulgating is the *Journal of the American Medical Association,* a highly respected medical periodical that gets quoted whatever it says, because it is so respected. I have never visited the offices of the *Journal of the American Medical Association,* but I suspect it is two guys named Murray and Ed, who sit around smoking cigars, playing practical jokes on each other, and inventing alarming facts. "Let's put it

---

1. This illustrates a psychological phenomenon known as "superstitious behavior." In one study, behavioral scientists placed a dozen pigeons in boxes and fed each bird pellets of food at completely random intervals, to see what would happen. After a few days, the pigeons were behaving bizarrely. One was hopping up and down on one foot; another was moving in circles with one wing raised; a third was incessantly scratching the wall, etc. The scientists eventually theorized that because there was no rhyme or reason to the feeding schedule, the birds had leaped to the conclusion that whatever they had just been doing immediately before they got a pellet—whatever random act—must have prompted the feeding. So they began doing that one thing more and more, and each time they were fed, it reinforced this belief. This is the only specific lesson I recall from four years as a psychology major in college.

out that laboratory rats are seventy percent more likely to develop esophageal cancer if spanked continually," Murray says. "No, wait," says Ed. "If spanked continually *while being fed a diet of Ovaltine and Snickers.*"

No one questions these studies, however preposterous they seem. I am looking at the results of a medical study recently reported by *The Washington Post*. Ordinarily, *The Washington Post* is pretty careful. If someone contended that President Chester Alan Arthur had actually been a donkey named Salvatore, you can bet the editors would demand a second source. But when a scientific study says something, newspapers instantly accept it because it is so darned scientific. This study I am looking at, solemnly reported by *The Washington Post* and other great newspapers, concludes that heart attacks might be prevented by diligent tooth flossing.

The media are the last and most important reason for the persistence of hypochondria in America. They'll print anything.

The New York Times recently reported that a cure for cancer was just around the corner, in the form of a new drug that can shrink tumors by cutting off their blood supply. Everyone went nuts. CURE FOR CANCER JUST AROUND CORNER, the newspapers said. Medical stocks soared! Poets rhapsodized! Dying millionaires offered researchers tens of millions of dollars to become human guinea pigs! It turns out the headlines were accurate in every way except for certain words: "Cure," "Cancer," "Just," "Around," and "Corner."

For one thing, so far the cure only works on mice. For another, the drug in question is partly synthesized from mouse urine, and at this point it takes two hundred quarts of mouse urine to extract a millionth of an ounce of the drug, which means you would basically have to force-feed a thousand mice a thousand gallons of Gatorade over a thousand years to get enough medicine to shrink a single hemorrhoid.

By the time all this qualifying data came out, however, the media had lost interest in CANCER CURE, moving on to yet another Big Medical Story, namely, KILLER ERECTIONS. Men who took Viagra, the new potency pill, were reported to be dying like germs in a jar of Listerine. Follow-up stories revealed, however, that these victims tended to be seventy-five-year-old guys who—suddenly invigorated after twenty years of sexual somnolence—bounded briskly out of bed and into the saddle. Presumably, they died of heart attacks, or of old-lady-style hairpins briskly inserted between the third and fourth rib.

The press also insists on reporting news of horrifying new diseases and shocking medical errors, terrifying the hypochondriac. Some of these so-called medical mistakes are, of course, exaggerated. For example, I am at this moment looking at an Associated Press story about how the parents of a five-year-old girl are suing a doctor in Texas who was supposed to perform an appendectomy on their daughter but instead removed one of her fallopian tubes. Sure, it *looks* bad for the doctor, but I think we must give him the benefit of the doubt. Perhaps he was unfamiliar with anatomy, and when he asked, "What is that?" and a nurse said, "A fallopian tube," he panicked and cut it off. *I* sure would. A fallopian tube does not sound like a good thing.

Still, these are aberrations. Bad medical news is not happening with greater frequency than in yesteryear. It is just that the press is far better at finding and reporting it. Let's say in 1841 a cholera epidemic wiped out half of Montana. The event would be covered six weeks later, as news trickled in. Journalism in that era was a lot more genteel. Information was disseminated only reluctantly, gradually, in manageable little bursts of increasing gravity, the way one might deliver bad news to an elderly aunt with a weak heart:

NEWS OF THE TERRITORIES

A Distressing Affair

CHOLERA OUTBREAK

MANY SERIOUS INDISPOSITIONS REPORTED

Fig Poultices Applied

OUR CO-RESPONDENT'S EYEWITNESS ACCOUNT

20,000 Dead

It is reliably reported by cable from our Co-respondent in the Northwestern Territorial Provinces, that contrary to more sanguine reports published elsewhere, the most Unfortunate Event has occurred of a medical nature. Horses were not affected. As could best be confirmed by press-time . . .

And so forth.

Hypochondriacs of earlier years did not even read these stories. In fact, no one read these stories. People bought newspapers for the ads, many of which featured products like Dr. Von Otherwise's Patented Lip Balm and Heart Tonic, which promised a cure for Neuralgia, The Vapors, Constipation, Dropsy, Quinsy, Fustulating Bronchitis, and Vomitacious Catarrh.

Nowadays, however, both medicine and the media are better. Hypochondriacs have much more to obsess over.

On June 23, 1997, for example, the American media and the American medical establishment conspired to perpetrate the greatest assault ever on hypochondriacs. On that day, the American Diabetes Association officially announced—and the media dutifully reported—that it had lowered the blood glucose levels necessary to diagnose a person as having diabetes. Overnight, they created a serious health problem for tens of thousands of people *who had not had a health problem the day before.* Every endocrinologist in America immediately purchased a second yacht.

Here's a recent newspaper story reporting the final days of convicted Virginia cop killer Roy Bruce Smith. Mr. Smith requested a last meal consisting of a glass of Welch's grape juice, one-eighth level teaspoon of Epsom salts, and unleavened bread made with olive oil. He had been eating nothing else for months. His lawyer disclosed that Mr. Smith believed many of the world's health problems, including cancer and diabetes, are caused by soy, and that to counter any ill effects, people should eat more foods containing magnesium, including Epsom salts and Rolaids. Mr. Smith spent the last month of his life bargaining with his cell mates for Rolaids. His biggest regret, he told his lawyer, was that he could not get this information out to the world. Also, he had figured out a way to achieve cold fusion. This secret, too, died with him. He was executed by a lethal injection of soy sauce.[2]

Now that all this information has been published in an actual book, I predict hypochondriacs all over the country will start gobbling Rolaids.

Not that that will save them from flesh-eating bacteria.

Remember flesh-eating bacteria? They entered the public consciousness a few years ago, more or less the way the AIDS virus enters the human body: right up the wazoo. Some doctor somewhere in some reputable medical journal reported that there was a microorganism that digests protein, and if it gets into an open wound it will, ahem, consume flesh. Pretty soon the responsible media got onto this story, quoting experts, prudently cautioning against panic, noting dispassionately that there was a germ out there that could, under certain conditions, **EAT YOUR FACE OFF.**

Instantly this reached the supermarket tabloids, in particular one supermarket tabloid called the *Weekly World News,* and that

---

2. Wouldn't that have been *great*?

pretty much was the ball game. The *Weekly World News* makes the *National Enquirer* look like Kant's *Critique of Pure Reason*. As I recall, the *Weekly World News* promptly informed America

that a **CANNIBAL MICROBE** was *ON THE*

RAMPAGE, turning ordinary humans into

BLOBS
OF
GOO.

I do not mean to disparage the *Weekly World News*. The *Weekly World News* is a fabulous newspaper. I say that as a knowledgeable journalist who has worked at several major American newspapers. Not one of them was cool enough to report a cure for cancer but put it on page 27, under a story about a man who eats cockroaches.

Once the tabloids got hold of the flesh-eating-bacteria story, hypochondriacs began to appear in their doctors' offices whimpering and pointing with horror at their zits.

This, of course, was silly. Ordinary-looking pimples do not remotely resemble the skin eruptions created by flesh-eating bacteria.

Ordinary-looking pimples resemble the skin eruptions caused by a malignant tumor of the adrenal gland.

CHAPTER SIX

Hypochondria
and
Me

When I was twelve years old, my classmate Kenneth told me that if your urine smelled funny after you ate asparagus it meant you had cancer of the larynx. This frightened me, even though I did not, technically, know where the larynx was. Kenneth said it was the "stomach bone."

After worrying in silence for a week and probing gingerly for signs of an enlarged stomach bone, I finally screwed up my courage and asked my mom, who informed me that some people's urine smells funny after they eat asparagus[1] and that it doesn't mean anything bad. So I owed Kenneth one. It proved easy. Kenneth was not a mental giant. I told him the Punic Wars were between the Phoenicians and "the Krauts," and he wrote this on a test.

Revenge, it is said, is sweet. Mine had a sour undertaste. From that moment on, I sensed in myself something unhealthy. Many things unhealthy, in fact. It was the first tentative awakening of

---

1. Mom was wrong, actually. Asparagus contains chemicals called methyl thioesters, which make *everyone's* urine smell funny. However, some people lack the smell receptors in their noses to detect the odor. Really. This raises the fascinating epistemological paradox: If an asparagus eater pees in a toilet but there is no one around with the appropriate smell receptors, does the pee stink?

what was to become a lifelong engagement with hypochondria. For much of my life I was a hypochondriac, and now I am cured. Disclosure of the details of my cure will provide the spectacular denouement of this book, rewarding the loyal reader with soul-shattering insights into the delicate nexus of the psychological, physiological, and spiritual roots of disease, not to mention an anecdote about unconscious people farting. But all that will come later. I will disclose this much right now: When chronic illnesses are cured, the cure often comes about incrementally, over time, without a single, dramatic, defining moment. But the cure for my hypochondria occurred on September 17, 1991, a Day That Will Live in Infirmity. It was shortly after ten o'clock[2] in the morning. It was a Tuesday. It was raining. God wept. But I am getting several chapters ahead of myself.

When I was thirteen, I began going to the dentist all the time, complaining of tooth pain. This was partly hypochondria, but mostly it was substance abuse. My dentist, whom I will call Dr. Bliss, had a practice that, as far as I could tell, consisted primarily of dispensing nitrous oxide. He would give you nitrous oxide to clean your teeth. He would give you nitrous oxide when he *examined* your teeth. He would give you nitrous oxide when he was in the other room, working on someone *else's* teeth. Dr. Bliss's patients—men, women, kids, blue-haired grandmas—would sit in his waiting room fidgeting and eyeing each other guiltily, like crack addicts.

Nitrous oxide is called laughing gas, though I never understood why. It never made me laugh. It was like sex: *waaaay* too intense to make you laugh, but hardly unenjoyable. Each time I was under nitrous oxide I would attain some overwhelming philosophical revelation that disappeared the instant I came out of the anesthesia. At this critical juncture, I once ripped off the rubber mask, grabbed a pen from the doctor's shirt pocket, and scribbled my insight onto my bib. This is what I wrote, in its entirety:

"I-N-G!!"

---

2. Did you ever wonder about the stupidity of the term "o'clock"? Americans have happily incorporated into our everyday speech a term that makes us sound like leprechauns.

In subsequent visits I honed this revelation, eventually determining that the meaning of life involved gerunds. But that is about as far as I got.[3] Personally, I think Dr. Bliss was everything you could want in a dentist, except that by the time I was sixteen, my molars were made entirely of ferrous compounds.

Though rooted in childhood, my hypochondria did not fully manifest itself until I was a young adult. For that I credit Dr. Katzev, my family doctor when I was a boy. Dr. Katzev was a crusty old guy who did not believe in pampering you or letting you pamper yourself. He was an ascetic. He believed absolutely in letting diseases take their natural course. Once, after he examined my brother, his diagnosis was: "If spots develop, it's the measles."

Dr. Katzev actually made house calls. He would barge into my bedroom, pull off the covers, and fling open the window, even if it was the dead of winter and I had a fever of 103. "The body has to breathe," he would say. Then he would instruct me to stop that infernal tooth chattering. To the best of my recollection, Dr. Katzev's diagnosis was always the same: I had a "bug" that was "going around."

(I would not have been surprised if years later Dr. Katzev achieved fame in one of those news stories you see from time to time where some kindly family physician, beloved by his patients, is discovered to be a refrigerator repairman.)

Dr. Katzev viewed all complaints skeptically. He did not cotton to drug therapy or fancy diagnostic tools. Mostly he used a stethoscope and one of those triangular reflex hammers. One day when I was seventeen, I went to Dr. Katzev complaining of a pain in the eye. He said, "If I hit you on the elbow with my hammer, your eye won't hurt so much."

Dr. Katzev urged me to keep an eye on the eye and see what

---

3. At least one kid got further. Around this time, a teenager broke into a dentist's office in Queens. His body was found the following day with a nitrous oxide mask on his face. I considered this one of the most significant stories of my generation, even though it was buried in the newspapers. Evidently, other news was deemed "more important." For years I remembered this as an example of the media's cowardice in dealing forthrightly with stories involving drugs and kids. Then, a few weeks ago, leafing through some old papers, I actually found the original news clipping. It was indeed buried deep in the paper. The date was November 22, 1963.

developed. I tried, though it became increasingly hard through the slime that was oozing over my eyeball. I continued watching carefully as a red rash developed around the eye, expanding into a weird, angry blotch that bisected my forehead right at the midline and ran down the center of my nose, veering off at a ninety-degree angle across my cheek. I looked like the victim of some sort of peculiar windburn, as if I were Mort—that character from *Bazooka Joe* comics who wears a turtleneck up over his mouth— and had driven the autobahn at 120 miles an hour with my head half out the window.

Reluctantly—no doubt suspecting that he was shamefully overreacting—Dr. Katzev finally sent me to a specialist, from whom I learned I had a serious viral disease called herpes zoster ophthalmicus. It attacks the nerves in your face around the eye. After the doctor told me his diagnosis, and that herpes zoster ophthalmicus usually clears up on its own, he went into another room and told my parents the same thing, adding something he hadn't thought wise to share with me: that herpes zoster ophthalmicus has been known to cause blindness, and there was no surefire way to prevent this.

So then my parents had to make a decision. On the one hand, being Jewish, they believed in the Talmudic principle of truth telling. On the other hand, being Jewish, they believed it is a mortal sin to cause one's son to worry. They decided to compromise.

Me: So I guess everything is going to be OK!

Them: Yes! Absolutely!

My Mother: *(whispering to my father in Yiddish)* Unless he goes blind like a burrowing rodent, the poor, sweet dumpling.

Me: *(to my father)* What did she say?

My Father: How do I know? I'm half deaf.

I recovered fine. If anything, the experience reinforced in me an appreciation of Dr. Katzev's laissez-faire medical philosophy. The disease *had* cleared up, on its own.

Then, in 1974, Dr. Katzev died of a cold.

I had loved and respected Dr. Katzev; he had always seemed wise and kind and indestructible, and in a generic, no-frills sort of way he had been a terrific family doctor. He cared about his patients. His death—caused by neglecting his sniffles and coughs until they turned into congestive heart failure[4]—made me aware of the importance of vigilance in maintaining good health. *Profoundly* aware.

I was twenty-three. Around that time I developed a pain in my jaw. I went to see a doctor. The doctor was stymied. Thinking aloud, he made an observation. It wasn't a diagnosis; he was simply making pleasant conversation, sharing his knowledge. He should writhe in hell for all eternity. What he said was that he had just read about a study of soldiers in World War I. If they came under hostile fire, they had been trained to fling themselves forward into a prone position, with their rifles flat out in front of them, at arm's length. Sometimes, a soldier's chin would come down on his rifle stock. And about a year later, this soldier would begin to experience undifferentiated pain in his jaw, not dissimilar to mine. Soon after that, his teeth would begin to fall out, one at a time, until he looked like Lamb Chop.

The doctor went on to describe other, more benign possible causes for my pain, but I wasn't hearing him. I was lost in an unimaginable terror. Had I suffered a minor blow to the chin a year before? Could be. I seemed maybe to recall something. I left his office feeling a spreading pain in my jaw, and for weeks afterward, it got worse. Night after night, I would examine my teeth in the mirror, shaking them, feeling to see if they were loose. Have you ever tried that? Try it now. Grab one of your lower front teeth and shake it. Feel that shimmy? It is normal. But you could not have convinced me of that.

I looked in the mirror, and the face that looked back at me was myself in a few months' time. Moms Mabley. I walked around shaking my teeth, feeling the pain creep from molar to molar. It

---

4. This was an ironic death, but it does not approach the one that befell Jim Fixx, the messianic jogging guru who had a massive heart attack while jogging. And Jim Fixx's death does not approach the most ironic demise of all time, suffered by one J. I. Rodale, the publisher of health and fitness books and founder of *Prevention* magazine. On June 7, 1971, Rodale was a guest on a late-night TV show. "I've never felt better in my life," he bragged. "I am so healthy that I expect to live on and on." Then he made a gurgling noise, pitched forward, and died.

lasted for months, until I got a great new job in an exciting new city. And rather suddenly, the pain went away.

Years passed, relatively complaint free. One day, I felt an ache in the groin. It started mildly but gradually became incapacitating.

I saw a series of urologists, none of whom could find anything wrong with me. Several of them prescribed medications; one of these, Urised, has the spectacular side effect of turning your urine blue. I do not mean cerulean blue, like the sky on a balmy summer day. Bic pen blue. Once, as I was standing at one of those trough urinals in a bathroom at a football stadium, I became aware that the man next to me was staring down at me, slack jawed. An opportunity like this occurs but once in life. I zipped up, pulled a cigarette lighter out of my pocket, and spoke into it in a robotic voice: "Gardak reporting. Earth colonization plans complete. Initiating return to mother ship."

Urised didn't relieve my problem. Nothing did. My doctor eventually asked me if I was having stress at work or in my home life.

I said no, not really. And he just stared at me. A thunderclap of silence. And finally I said, "Well, except my girlfriend wants to get married and have a baby and I think the company I work for might be about to go bankrupt, plus I have no talent, no integrity, and no future."

And the doctor gave me his diagnosis: "You are a young man. Enjoy your life."

And the pain went away.

Clearly, a pattern was emerging.

Over the years, I had a rather civil relationship with my hypochondria. Each time a symptom would arise, I would consult a doctor—or sometimes two because the first guy was obviously an incompetent. No cause would be found, I would conclude the pain must have been psychosomatic, and it would go away. Each time, however, I had to first become convinced it was something dreadful, because by doing so I would be mentally prepared for the Bad News when it arrived. I think this is at the heart of hypochondria: a fear of losing control in the face of adversity. The hypochondriac resents the arbitrary nature of death. He wants control. And control comes with knowledge.

And so, when I felt light-headed for a month, I leafed through some books and determined it was multiple sclerosis. Stomach pain was an ulcer, and when it did not respond to ulcer medication it was stomach cancer. Once, the skin on my hands began to peel. This was a tough one. Medical books suggest no obvious alarming causes of skin peeling. I eventually found one. It took a little research, but hypochondriacs are not averse to research. It turns out skin peeling is often caused by excessive localized sweating, and excessive localized sweating, *particularly of the hands,* can in rare instances indicate a brain tumor. For days I sucked on my fingers to see if they tasted abnormally salty. This, of course, made the peeling worse. I was eventually cured of this illness by getting a raise.

My own physiology became a subject of endless fascination and terror. I began noticing the floaters in my eye, those harmless, diaphanous shapes that sometimes swim around your field of vision, turning your eyes into snow globes, only without the Statue of Liberty in the middle.[5]

Most people have floaters, but they don't notice them until one day they do. Then they notice nothing else. That's what happened to me. Before I had noticed my floaters, a pastoral scene would look like this:

---

5. Unless, of course, you happen to be looking at the Statue of Liberty.

Once I had noticed my floaters, the same scene looked like this:

Hypochondria is not communicable, but it is transferable. And so it is that when my daughter began getting headaches and an ophthalmologist looked into her eyes and determined that she had an odd bulging of her optic nerves, I did some quick research and concluded she had pressure on the brain caused by a tumor. Painfully, I rehearsed how I would tell her, how I would make her final months as comfortable as possible. Tentatively, I began to write my speech for her funeral, which was to be more a symphony than a dirge—a celebration of a remarkable young life, heroically lived. Practically, I weighed the financial ramifications: readjusting what we are salting away for college tuitions. Selflessly, I resolved to inquire about whether my employer offered bereavement leave and to make it a union issue if the company did not, as a way to harness my grief for the benefit of others. This all occurred in about twelve minutes. It turned out my daughter's problem was a harmless medical condition defined, more or less, as "big fat optic nerves."

To the hypochondriac, actual crises involving loved ones come as something of a respite, because they take his mind off his troubles. Plus, when illness does strike in the family, the hypochondriac is *much* better prepared to handle it. He's been in training his whole life.

One winter day a few years ago, on a dare from me, my nine-year-old son, Dan, was sledding down Dead Man's Hill. He hit a bump, rose into the air, and came down like a moose dropped from a helicopter. He bit clean through his lower lip. We took him to the hospital, where a plastic surgeon informed us he was going to operate, right then.

At times like this, my wife and I employ a careful division of labor. My wife's job is to walk away so she doesn't faint. My job, as the resident hypochondriac, is to wade hip deep into the disaster. In this case, my job was to stand over Dan and act jolly so he could not possibly guess what the doctor was doing. What the doctor was doing was gouging out a huge bubbling basin in Dan's face, making the hole much wider and deeper so the incision line would be even, as opposed to the incision line made by one's teeth, which looks like something gnawed by a starving ferret. The operation was so alarming I actually removed my glasses so there was no chance Dan might see a reflection in the lenses and puke into the foxhole that was his face.

But I remembered the lesson I had learned from my parents all those years before. I didn't want to lie to my son, even with a lie of omission. So I kept up a constant drone of happy, insipid, mind-deadening babble, things like, "Yo, Dan, that was a hell of a hill, wasn't it, big feller, ha ha! I'll bet Mom is plenty pissed at me, ha ha! Your lip looks like a baboon's anus, ha ha!"

Dan pulled through with barely a scar, but the experience took a toll on me. By the time I got home, I had a splitting headache.

Encephalitis, I was pretty sure.

CHAPTER SEVEN

Hiccups
Can Mean
Cancer

---

*I*n *many ways* the human body is like a car. Both are complex machines. Both require regular maintenance. Both will stop working if you fill them with barbiturates and applesauce.

Having a car and having a body both require adherence to a rigid servicing schedule. Let's say you own a car and you never, ever replace the oil; and when you use jumper cables, you get them mixed up and there is a spark the size of the Crab nebula, draining all the juice out of the good battery; and once, you poured windshield wiper fluid into the power steering reservoir because they really should label these things better. My point is, if you are that much of a half-wit about your car, your car is the least of your problems, because you probably also use a hair dryer in the bathtub.

The fact is, both cars and humans are designed with idiot lights, things that alert the reasonably careful person that something serious is awry. If your car's *Oil* light goes on, unless you are my wife, you probably know to stop driving and see a mechanic at once. Similarly, if you experience serious chest pains, then you probably will see a doctor. The fact is, certain symptoms are by their nature scary. Lumps. High fever. Blood in the stool. Mental confusion.[1]

This chapter is not about those common "warning signals." This chapter is about things no sane person would ever associate with serious illness, until this very moment.

Hiccups. The precise cause (or "etiology") of hiccups remains a matter of some dispute among medical scientists, who have studied the phenomenon incessantly and come away with only obvious clinical observations, such as that men hiccup, on the average, five times as frequently as women. (As far as I can see, this tends to suggest, in sophisticated medical terms, an "etiology" related to beer.) There is no reliable cure for hiccups, but there is no shortage of nostrums available, each with its adherents. The rule of thumb is that the more unpleasant the remedy, the more august is the medical authority recommending it. Grandma told you to hold your breath. *Primary Care Medicine,* a text for doctors, proposes inserting a catheter down your nose into your stomach. I recommend hyperventilating into a colostomy bag.

Hiccups are harmless, except when they aren't. No other commonly reported symptom has quite so many potentially dire explanations. Persistent hiccups cross into virtually every medical specialty. Neurologists know hiccups can accompany the onset of a deadly stroke or an inoperable tumor in the medulla of the brain. Cardiologists will not rule out an oncoming heart attack or an aortic aneurysm. Nephrologists will suspect kidney failure. Gastroenterologists know hiccups can indicate an "irritation" of the diaphragm or of some other organ, particularly one that touches the vagus or phrenic nerves, which control the swallowing and breathing reflexes.

---

1. Of course, if you are mentally confused, you might not *realize* you are mentally confused. That is the nature of mental confusion. You could be mentally confused right now. You could be thinking you are reading this book, but in fact, you are *remembering* having read this book in your youth. It could be the year 2049 and you are ninety-five years old in a nursing home, rocking back and forth in your own incontinence. If you suspect this may be the case, here is a way to test: Remove your pants. If someone comes to help you, you are probably in a nursing home. If people sort of shrink away from you, you are probably on the subway or something and everything is OK.

On the outside of the body, an irritation is often a minor matter. On the inside, it often isn't. On the inside, it is often a tumor. Hiccups have been associated with tumors in or around the lung, in the diaphragm, the liver, the pancreas, the stomach, and even the sigmoid colon, which is down near the butt and should not, by the grace of God, have anything to do with breathing.

Insomnia. In the absence of other symptoms, excessive fatigue or excessive sleep can be an indication of many serious diseases, but insufficient sleep generally isn't. Most of the time, the insomniac knows or suspects why he can't sleep: He is worried or depressed, or he has a toothache, or asthma, or a goiter the size of a microwave oven. Insomnia seldom stands alone, but when it does, it is out there in the hellish regions of Things You Wouldn't Wish on Your Worst Enemy Even If He Ate Garbo, Your Dachshund.

The most dramatic of these is fatal familial insomnia. This is a disease caused by prions, which are proteins that act exactly like ice-nine, the instrument of the apocalypse in Kurt Vonnegut's *Cat's Cradle*. Ice-nine was a molecular template. If it mixed with water, it would turn the water molecules into ice-nine molecules, rock hard and useless for sustaining life. This was not good when it spread across the oceans of the world. That's how prions work. They get into your body and take other proteins and reorder their structure to resemble themselves. In fatal familial insomnia, prions take up residence in the sleep center of your brain and slowly destroy it. You start out being unable to sleep well. Then you cannot sleep at all. In desperation, you see a top neurologist like Dr. Anthony Reder of the University of Chicago.

A few years ago, a man came to see Dr. Reder. The patient was tired and grouchy—not tired and grouchy like a bus driver at the end of his route, but tired and grouchy like the people from *Invasion of the Body Snatchers* immediately before the dull-eyed pods took them over. This patient looked disheveled. His hair was askew, like Beethoven's after a night of carousing. Reder had seen this before; he is a research scientist and had seen it in laboratory rats with sleep deprivation. He diagnosed fatal familial insomnia. There is no treatment. There was nothing that could be done. Within weeks, the patient was hallucinating, making up grandiose stories about himself. His appearance deteriorated. Beethoven lost a lot of his charm. He gave way to Dr. Irwin Corey. Then he died.

Laughing So Hard You Pee in Your Pants. There is actually a medical term for this. Urologists call it "giggle incontinence." It can mean nothing, or it can be a very early indication of neurologic disease, in particular multiple sclerosis.

The Sniffles. Sometimes a cold is nothing to sneeze at. It could be the first sign of Wegener's granulomatosis, a rare, fulminant, whole-system body breakdown that often starts with coughing, congestion, and blood-streaked nasal discharge. Looks just like a cold! Then, when it doesn't go away, it looks like chronic bronchitis, maybe with an ear infection. Small wonder that Wegener's granulomatosis is sometimes not properly diagnosed until it is too late to treat. By that time it has progressed to kidney failure, lung damage, and body deformities, including "saddle nose," in which the nose cartilage collapses like a rotted jack-o'-lantern.

Or your "cold" might mean you have anthrax. Anthrax is a bacillus carried by livestock; an airborne, inhaled form of it starts just like a cold. This is relatively rare, though terrorist states like Iraq are experimenting with it as a biological weapon. They are planning to use it against citizens of decadent Western regimes, in cities and towns very much like yours. A doomsday scenario? Yes. Far-fetched? Hardly. The armed services have begun a program to inoculate soldiers against airborne anthrax. When inhaled, anthrax resembles the flu for a day or two, and then you feel pretty good, as if your cold has waned. Three days pass. Then you start hacking uncontrollably, you perspire like a federal witness against the mob, and finally you turn as blue as Cookie Monster. It is nearly 100 percent fatal.

Ringing in the Ears. This is called "tinnitus." Most people experience tinnitus at one time or another, usually as a high-pitched whine, but sometimes as a buzzing, whooshing, or clanging. Usually it is harmless. Sometimes the sounds can be heard by the doctor when she places a stethoscope to your ear, and this generally means it is no cause for alarm. It is when you are hearing the sounds and she is not that she[2] begins to get concerned. Other possibilities open up, some harmless, some worrisome. It can mean Ménière's disease, a disorder of the inner ear. That would be comparatively good news; Ménière's disease is usually controllable by medication. Tinnitus can also sometimes signal multiple sclerosis, or it can accompany the first appearance of a growth on the brain stem or auditory nerve known as a "schwannoma." A schwannoma is not usually malignant, but it is not entirely harmless, either; sometimes, when it is surgically removed, facial nerves are damaged and you wind up with a perpetual snotty look on your face, like a French wine connoisseur who has been asked to evaluate Yoo-Hoo. A schwannoma also presents the practitioner with a diagnostic dilemma: How do you deliver the news to a patient that he has a tumor with a name that sounds as if you are calling him a penis-head? Come to think of it, perhaps that is why it is named a schwannoma. Maybe doctors are learning to give silly-sounding names to terrifying things to ease the tension of the diagnosis. Maybe soon they will rename a heart attack a "spankadoodle."

Cold Sores and Fever Blisters. That eruption on your lip or gums probably means a minor attack from the herpes simplex virus. No big deal. Keep it clean. Use a mouthwash. It will go away, unless it is the initial presentation of pemphigus vulgaris, a disease that is even worse than it sounds. Pemphigus begins as mouth blisters—weeping, bleeding, painful,

---

2. Note the somewhat jarring use of the female pronoun. This is a brilliant preemptive strike against those who will later question the author's gender sensitivity, such as in Chapter 16, when he describes a colleague's hooters.

funky-smelling sores that spread to the skin of your scalp and elsewhere. Pemphigus can be treated and controlled but seldom is cured outright. One of the better experimental treatments involves injections of gold. It is expensive.

Pins and Needles. You say, "My foot fell asleep." Your doctor says, "You have experienced a transient episode of paresthesia." Either way, you are standing there on two feet, but one feels like a shillelagh being nibbled by carpenter ants. The usual explanation is that you sat wrong, compressing a nerve. And that's probably what happened, unless your pins and needles are the deceptively lilting overture of Guillain-Barré syndrome, a mysterious, terrifying disorder of the peripheral nerves. It starts in the foot, with sensations indistinguishable from ordinary pins and needles. Then it rapidly distinguishes itself, in the sense that a letter from the Unabomber rapidly distinguishes itself from the rest of the mail. The pins and needles will give way to profound muscle weakness. You can't lift an arm; sometimes you can't even breathe without the help of a respirator. Your brain is fine but your body is a dull lump of useless protoplasm—sort of the opposite of Vanna White. Most people eventually recover. From then on, whenever their foot falls asleep, they do not take it lightly. They worry, waiting for the next development, on pins and needles.

Itching. Doctors call this "pruritus," which makes it sound vaguely dirty and exciting. Alas, it is just itching. When itching is localized, the diagnosis is relatively simple. Seborrhea, psoriasis, dermatitis, athlete's foot, ringworm, scabies, lice.[3] It is when itching is generalized that all sorts of possibilities arise. If it is centered in the feet or the lower half of the body, it can be one of the first signs of Hodgkin's disease, a potentially fatal cancer of the lymphatic system. Generalized itching can signal a form of leukemia. It can be the very first symptom of lung cancer, ovarian cancer, pancreatic cancer, or

---

3. True fact: The official medical terminology for having lice is "lousiness."

prostate cancer. It is almost always the first symptom of Hanot's cirrhosis, a life-threatening liver disease of middle-aged women. And then there is mycosis fungoides, the final ring of itching hell.

Mycosis fungoides is a rare, galloping skin tumor. It starts with itching; you ignore it. Then, sometimes, years go by symptom-free. Then the itching returns with a vengeance. Then your body erupts into patchy discolorations. You resemble a dalmatian. Then the discolorations spread. You resemble a guernsey cow. Then the tumors become what the medical books describe as "tomatolike." Then things start getting *really* ugly . . .

Déjà Vu. We are all familiar with this peculiar existential phenomenon. Suddenly, irrationally, we feel we are experiencing an event, or hearing a conversation, that we have experienced before. There is another, similar condition, called "jamais vu," in which the opposite occurs: You suddenly feel that familiar surroundings are foreign to you; you might not even recognize your spouse. Cool. Weird. Potentially deadly. Neurologists have discovered that déjà vu and jamais vu can be early signs of a tumor or hemorrhage in the temporal lobe of the cerebral cortex.

Troubled by these mental hiccups? Look for additional subtle signs of temporal lobe abnormalities. One would be seizures. If you frequently find yourself waking up on the floor at work in a pool of urine, with a gnawed pencil in your teeth, and people standing around trying to look calm, you may have a problem here.[4]

---

4. Speaking of seizures, I cannot forbear mentioning the story, recently reported in the *Emergency Physicians Monthly,* of the attractive couple in dinner attire who came into an emergency room in Spokane, Washington, he with his loins wrapped in bloody towels, she wearing what appeared to be a bloody turban. The man's penis had deep lacerations, and the woman's head had many severe puncture wounds, in odd cluster patterns. Initially reluctant to discuss what had happened, the couple eventually fessed up: After a romantic candlelit dinner and some excellent merlot, the woman decided to perform an exceedingly friendly service to her companion, under the table. Midway through, she suffered an epileptic seizure, clamping down the way a terrier might attack a rat. That is when he reached for the fork . . .

Flushed Face. People sometimes get red in the face. This can be caused by exertion or emotion, or by profound embarrassment, such as when you are at a podium to address a national group of educators and you suddenly realize that the big exuberant German shepherd you were petting a few minutes before has nosed you in the lap so enthusiastically that you have an enormous frothy wet spot on the portion of your beige silk dress roughly corresponding to your own personal groin, not that this ever happened to anyone I know.[5] Flushing can also be caused by drinking alcohol. Sometimes this is normal, but sometimes flushing after drinking alcohol is an early warning sign of carcinoid syndrome, in which tumors invade the lining of the stomach; this alcohol-induced facial flushing can precede the diagnosis by fifteen years! By that time, tumors have often spread to the liver or bone or another system. You have fire-hose diarrhea. Your heart walls thicken. You get short of breath. Then short of time.

Hoarseness. This is how lung cancer sometimes shows up for the first time; the tumor invades the laryngeal nerve and you suddenly sound like Vito Corleone.

Lipstick on Your Teeth. Yes, this is potentially serious. The canny internist will not discount this symptom. It suggests dry mucous membranes. If it tends to happen on one side of your mouth only, it could be due to a tumor of cranial nerve VII, which supplies the salivary glands. But the same eye would probably also be dry. If your entire mouth is dry and you are not taking any drugs that dry you out, this could be an early indication of Sjogren's syndrome, an autoimmune disease that generally affects menopausal or postmenopausal Caucasian women.

5. Carol Scheman, Philadelphia, Pennsylvania.

Doctors will sometimes ask a patient to eat two saltines without water; Sjogren's victims cannot do it.

Sjogren's syndrome can lead to tooth rot, sexual dysfunction, and greater susceptibility to lymphatic cancers. There are support groups for victims of Sjogren's syndrome. They are mostly women in middle age. They are very careful with their lipstick.

The Blahs. You don't feel good. You can't quite put your finger on it. You are weak and achy and maybe you have a slight sore throat or fever. Medically, this is "malaise," and it usually means a cold is coming on. Some serious ailments begin this way, too, the most terrifying of which may be Stevens-Johnson syndrome, or erythema multiforme. You start by just feeling crappy. Soon there are eruptions on the lips, the tongue, and the inside of the mouth. You blister horribly. It spreads to the genitals and, sometimes, the anus. Sometimes you go blind. Here is how bad it is: Sometimes the only place that can treat you is a hospital burn unit.

Words on the Tip of Your Tongue. It is called "partial anomia" or "tip-of-the-tongue phenomenon." You find yourself having increasing trouble retrieving the right, er, er, er . . . word. It could just mean benign forgetfulness: As you get older, memory and retrieval functions sometimes get a little impaired. But neurologists know partial anomia can be an early sign of several degenerative dementias. It occurs with the onset of tumors in the left hemisphere of the brain, or in metabolic disturbances typical of terminal liver disease. It can also be the very, very tip of the very, very cold iceberg known as er, er, er . . . Alzheimer's.

Nausea. Having nausea in the absence of vomiting is like drinking NutraSweet in the absence of Diet Coke. What's the point? Fortunately, simple lack of appetite coupled with a vague nausea that doesn't make you puke is seldom a serious symptom. Unfortunately, when it *is* a serious symptom, what it is a symptom of is an oncoming heart attack.

Snorting Out Food. You are dining on, say, spaghetti carbonara. Someone tells a joke, but not just any joke. It must be a joke with a certain kind of punch line: a bad-boy punch line, unexpected and a little wicked, like the one about why women don't skydive naked.[6] Suddenly you've got pasta and bacon dribbling out of your nose. Now, maybe you are just a slob, but possibly you have a degenerative disease in the muscles served by the cranial nerves. In the early stages, these conditions can cause the sudden, startling nasal regurgitation of food or drink. The later stages make the sudden, startling nasal regurgitation of food or drink seem like the height of prandial etiquette.

Bad Breath. Medical texts first warn you, in medical-text language, that the most likely cause of bad breath is crummy dental hygiene. The catchall medical term for organisms that cause your breath to stink is "oral flora." As in, "Yo, Vinnie, stand downwind on account of your oral flora is making me want to puke up this here sausage." Once bad breath has been eliminated as a cause of bad breath, the physiology gets much more interesting, and specific. A musty, fishy odor or, alternatively, a sickeningly sweet odor could be an early sign of terminal liver failure. A light, fruity odor could mean ketoacidosis, a condition that frequently accompanies diabetes. An odor of ammonia could mean nephritic gingivitis, a mouth-and-gum disease linked to incipient kidney failure. A stench of rotting garbage could mean lung disease. A smell of sweaty feet or cheese can indicate a serious metabolic disorder. A smell of garlic may be a sign of poisoning by arsenic, selenium, tellurium, or phosphorus. However, all of these things are likely to be accompanied by other signs, such as fatigue,

---

6. I bet you thought I was going to give you the punch line here.

mouth sores, a bloody cough, jaundiced skin, or extreme thirst.

There is only one serious ailment for which bad breath alone can be the initial sign that something is wrong—though people seldom seek help at this early stage. Who wants to arrive at the doctor complaining that you smell like a septic tank? So you wait. Eventually, you get a persistent earache. Or congestion in one nostril. That's when you discover you have a squamous cell carcinoma of the throat or sinus. The prognosis often stinks.

Yawning. One of the great mysteries of medicine is why yawns are contagious. The fact that they are is often cited as evidence that yawning itself is without clinical significance; if it can be induced by mere suggestion, how can it mean anything bad? This is good reasoning, but alas, it is wrong. Paroxysms of yawning or sighing in the absence of real fatigue can be an early sign of encephalitis, or of a tumor or hemorrhage in the central part of the brain. These things push the brain downward, making it ooze through into areas where the brain has no business being, and for some reason this process can induce yawning, sighing, and later, stupor and death. This condition is called a "central herniation," or an "uncal herniation." It is very bad. Maybe someone should write a children's book featuring a character named Uncle Herniation. He would be sort of like Sleepy the Dwarf, only he'd keep getting crushing headaches, spinal fluid would run out of his nose, and in the end he would lapse into a coma and die.

Nosebleeds. If you go to a doctor complaining of nosebleeds, he will first make vague, discreet inquiries, using big, dignified words like "extrusion," and it will slowly dawn on you that he is asking you if you pick your nose. The fact is, the capillaries in the nose are a threadwork of vessels easily damaged by, say, a pinkie.[7] After ruling this out, and ruling out obvious

---

7. Why do you suppose we have a name for each of our fingers, but not for each of our toes? It seems wrong. I propose that the toes be named as follows, from the largest to the smallest: Big Wally, Shitkicker, Old Number Three, Gruntcakes, and Thor.

other genetic causes you will probably know about—hemophilia, for example—the doctor will begin looking for diseases you don't know about: These include a series of things with very long names. One is an esoneuroblastoma. Another is a nasopharyngeal angiofibroma. These are nasal tumors, and they tend to debut as nosebleeds.

If these immediate causes of your nosebleed are eliminated, the doctor will consider systemic causes, diseases that affect your whole body but first show as nosebleeds. One would be an inflammation of the right side of the heart. Or the doctor might suspect Waldenström's macroglobulinemia, a blood disease that is terrifying not only because it turns you weak, pale, and blind, and then tends to kill you, but because it involves the use of an umlaut, which makes everything sound worse than it is. Try it. Settle a few umlauts atop the most benign thing you can imagine, and watch what happens: Sänta Claüs. The jolly patron of Nazi children.

But a more likely explanation for nosebleeds would be cirrhosis. You don't have to be a drunk to get cirrhosis. Liver disease can sneak up on you, and sometimes you can be near death before you notice anything is wrong. One warning signal is that the liver stops doing what it is supposed to do, including helping the body absorb vitamin K, which helps blood to clot. If there isn't enough, you bleed. It can start with the capillaries in your nose. This is the early stage. Eventually, you cough and vomit up huge gobs of cherry red, clumpy blood the consistency of rice pudding. Sometimes it will be darker and look like chicken livers or coffee grounds. This stage of your disease is called "hematemesis." People with terminal cirrhosis don't get invited to many parties.

Snoring. You snore at night and feel tired during the day. You are a man. You are middle aged. You are at least somewhat overweight. You might have obstructive sleep apnea, a serious sleep disorder in which the pharynx collapses and prevents you from breathing. This can last up to two minutes without waking you. Your heart rhythm is impaired. Your body is starved for oxygen, a condition called hypoxia. The brain hates this; it degenerates, and so do you. Your family notices changes in personality; you get cranky and irritable and, according to medical texts, you "show poor judgment at work."[8] Untreated, this can lead to cor pulmonale, a condition that destroys the heart's right ventricle. You become impotent. You look sort of purple. The veins in your neck pop out, resembling a hangman's rope. By then, you want to die. Sometimes you do.

What can be done? First, a doctor will have to determine whether you actually have sleep apnea; some people are just fat, cranky boors with bad judgment. If the diagnosis is sleep apnea, there is an operation called uvulopalatopharyngoplasty (we'll just call it "Bob"), in which the whole back of your throat is sheared off. Usually this solves the problem. Sometimes it doesn't. You still snore and choke, only it hurts more because some idiot sheared your throat open.

Toothache. Get a bunch of dentists together in a room. Get them talking. Then get the hell out of there; there is nothing quite so stultifying as a room full of talking dentists. However, if you leave a tape recorder in the room, you can later fast-forward to the good parts. If he has practiced long enough, every dentist will have a story of a patient who complained of a toothache in the lower jaw. The teeth will look fine. But the patient won't. He will have clammy skin. The dentist will send him to the emergency room. That is because an emergency room is a better place than a dentist's office to have a massive coronary.

At other times, a patient will come in complaining of pain in the molars. An X-ray will reveal an ameloblastoma, a tumor of the bone in the lower jaw, in the wisdom tooth area. This is what is known as an "insidious" tumor. It grows slowly and causes no pain until it is quite large and crowds against the root of a tooth. By that time, the only solution may be removal

---

8. The medical books do not specify the nature of the poor judgment you might exhibit in the workplace. For the sake of medical accuracy, we will hypothesize that you wear only a cummerbund and a sombrero, conduct animal sacrifices in the employees' lounge, and address the boss as Puny Mortal.

of all or part of the lower jaw. A prosthesis is inserted. It is usually part metal and part bone shaved from your hip. Depending on the skill of the surgeon, you might look pretty good, or you might look like Grover Cleveland. Cleveland had a jaw tumor; doctors removed a portion of the jaw and replaced it with vulcanized rubber. He was an excellent president but resembled a warthog.

Stiff Neck. "I probably just slept on it wrong." Yes, yes. Probably. In the last half century, the simple stiff neck has lost most of its cachet, due to advances in modern medicine. In the absence of other symptoms, waking up with a stiff neck used to be a first sign of polio or tetanus. But these days everyone is inoculated against polio. Also tetanus. You *have* had a tetanus shot, and a booster in the last five years, right? Not sure? You may wish to call your doctor. Ask him. If you sound like Thurston Howell IV, you may be in trouble. Doctors call this initial stage "trismus," or lockjaw. It will be rapidly followed by a ghastly grin that makes you look like the Joker. Doctors call this "risus sardonicus." Then your body bends backward, taut, like a crossbow. Doctors call this "opisthotonos." Doctors have a term for everything. If treatment is delayed, the final symptom can be "cessation of vital signs." Doctors call this "death."

CHAPTER EIGHT

Headaches:
Don't Worry, They're All
in Your Head

For some reason we tend to impart profound significance to a person's final words, as though God chooses to speak through the mouths of those He is about to summon. There have been some splendid deathbed pronouncements (Oscar Wilde is reputed to have said, "Either that wallpaper goes, or I do"), but alas, exit lines tend to be banal ("Shit!"), incomprehensible ("Gaack"), or memorably idiotic. Who can forget the immortal last words uttered by Civil War general John Sedgwick as he ridiculed his troops for taking cover from Confederate fire: "Come, come! Why, they couldn't hit an *elephant* at this dis—"

For hypochondriacs there is only one final line worth remembering, and it has given them the willies for more than a half century. On April 12, 1945, in Warm Springs, Georgia, Franklin Roosevelt turned to a friend and said: "I have a terrific headache." Then he slipped into a coma and died of a brain hemorrhage, which normal people call a stroke but doctors call an "accident."[1]

"I have a terrific headache" remains the anthem of the

---

1. See next chapter, on ridiculous medical euphemisms.

hypochondriac, who knows in his heart that headaches can and sometimes do signal the presence of a brain tumor or a stroke. Here is where an unfortunate irony of human anatomy comes into play. The brain is made of nerve tissue, but, perversely, it has no pain receptors. So, chances are you won't feel a stroke or a tumor when it first arrives; you will have to wait until it kicks off its shoes, reaches for the remote, and starts porking up on Doritos. Eventually it gets so fat it presses on vascular nerves, which causes a headache, or presses on other brain tissue, which can cause seizures, partial paralysis, or some of the weirdest danged things you ever saw. Tumors or bleeding can create personality changes ranging from irritability to confusion to confabulation, a strange state in which you compensate for memory loss by inventing an entire, elaborately detailed, improbable history for yourself. Asked, for example, if you have ever been married, you might say, "I was married for a time to Queen Fredericka of the Netherlands. She has three nipples."

Headaches are the single most reported medical symptom, and they have always been related to environmental stresses; headaches have gone hand in hand with the march of civilization. In prehistoric times, they were caused by persons hitting you on the head with the femur of an ox. During the Dark Ages, they were caused by being hung upside down in dungeons. In the Renaissance, people got headaches because they were tormented by anguish over the beastly unfairness of life. During the French Revolution, people got headaches because their hair weighed two hundred pounds, plus they wore quarts of perfume to disguise the fact that, as French people, they never bathed. In the Industrial Revolution, people got headaches because they were breathing air made from vaporized rubber and despair. In the 1920s people got headaches because they drank gin made in toilets from any available source of carbohydrates, such as corncobs, maggots, and pumpernickel. Through the 1950s, women got headaches because they did not wish to have sex with their husbands. (Thankfully, this artifice is no longer necessary, since conjugal "duties" are now an antiquated notion. Today, if a woman chooses not to have sex with her husband, she is no longer required to come up with an excuse. She can simply cut off his penis.)

Nowadays, doctors specializing in the treatment of headaches will tell you that most headaches are minor matters. Then their brows will furrow with professional concern; they will get a far-away look in their eyes and they will say, "Of course, there are exceptions. Notable, grave exceptions." You think doctors who specialize in headaches want you to walk out the door?

The hypochondriac doesn't have to be told that headaches can be related to tumors or strokes. He knows this. He also understands that headaches can signal encephalitis and meningitis, serious infections of the brain. There are some things he doesn't know, however. A crushing headache can be the first sign of cysticercosis. That is a parasitic disease in which the brain is infested by the larva of an intestinal tapeworm, *Taenia solium,* which can grow to twenty feet long.[2] In your brain, though, these worms are only a half inch long. Some people have both at the same time: huge ravenous worms in their guts, and small brain-burrowing worms in their head, which happens to throb quite a bit, just like with an ordinary headache, at first.

Cysticercosis is relatively rare in the United States. So, relax: Your headache is probably not caused by worms in your brain. It is more likely to be related to your consumption of mouse urine. (See chart below and follow-up questions.)

---

2. To get a mental picture of a twenty-foot tapeworm, imagine eating pasta by sucking a single strand noisily through your mouth. Now imagine that the strand turns out to be so long it takes you a full minute of nonstop sucking to get it down. Now imagine that when you get to the end you discover a face, with little feelers and a pair of googly eyes on stalks. There's your tapeworm! Worms have been turning up in surprising places since the worldwide sushi craze began ten years ago. In a case recently reported in the *New England Journal of Medicine,* surgeons performing an emergency appendectomy on a patient with abdominal pain were chagrined to find a perfectly normal appendix. Then a ten-inch pink worm slithered out from the body onto the surgical sheets.

Symptom	Possible Diagnosis	Look For	Prognosis
Headache with pain on chewing	Giant cell arteritis	Scalp tenderness	Can cause blindness.
Headache in obese young women	Pseudotumor cerebri	Double vision	Can cause blindness, ulcers, cataracts, breast atrophy, and diminished libido. Treatable through repeated spinal taps or oral corticosteroids, which makes the fat patient even fatter.
Headache with nasal congestion	Primary amebic meningoencephalitis, spread by polluted water	Vomiting; disorientation	Quickly fatal. In all medical history, only two people have survived it.
Headache with inability to focus eyes upward	Tumor of pineal gland[3]	Nausea; vomiting; clumsy, widened walking gait	Can delay onset of puberty for years. Can metastasize and result in death.
Headache with malaise	Bornholm disease ("devil's-grip")	Excessive sweating; fever; stitch in side	Lasts 2–6 days, but residual malaise can last for months. Men can develop swelling of testicles.
Headache with sore throat and depression	Benign myalgic encephalomyelitis	Numbness of legs	Persists for a month, with total flaccid paralysis of legs. May recur periodically.
Headache with dizziness, fatigue, and ringing in ears	Polycythemia rubra vera	Nosebleeds; itching, especially after a warm bath	Leads to ulcers, bleeding in the stomach, baseball-sized lumps at joints. Can lead to leukemia.

---

3. The pineal gland, in the brain, appears to have no clearly defined function other than to develop tumors. We will hypothesize that the pineal gland is the brain's highly efficient storehouse of annoying, obsolete information, such as the American Dental Association's declaration that Crest has been shown to be an effective decay-preventive dentifrice that can be of significant value when used in a conscientiously applied program of oral hygiene and regular professional care.

Symptom	Possible Diagnosis	Look For	Prognosis
Sudden, sharply focused headache	Saccular cerebral aneurysm	Nausea; vomiting	Sometimes fatal if it ruptures.
Headache with dry cough	Mycoplasmic pneumonia	Fever; malaise	Can develop into Guillain-Barré paralysis, heart swelling, and serious blistering of skin.
Throbbing headache with nausea and confusion	Carbon monoxide poisoning from faulty car exhaust or home furnace	Coma; seizures; cherry red lips	Full recovery if source of poisoning found in time; sometimes depression lingers, with memory impairment.
Headache that is most painful in the morning then slowly abates through the day	Severe hypertension	Wheezing; coughing	Can lead to heart attack, congestive heart failure, strokes, blindness, death.

And finally, some answers to commonly asked scientific questions about headaches.

I have a splitting headache and my muscles hurt and I feel kind of stoned and confused. It is possible I have been drinking mouse urine?

Yes. You are exhibiting symptoms of Weil's disease, or leptospirosis. It is spread by the urine of pigs and rodents, particularly mice and rats. You can pick it up from unclean food or water. Most people recover, but some will first turn a pale yellow. This is particularly unnerving, under the circumstances.

What is the stupidest official medical name for a headache?

There are two. The first is "Chinese restaurant syndrome headache," linked to consumption of monosodium glutamate. The second is "ice cream headache," caused by the sudden ingestion of very cold food, which aggravates the trigeminal nerve. These conditions are so dumb and harmless they do not have more technical, Latin names. And so "Chinese restaurant syndrome headache" and "ice cream headache" are listed soberly in the indexes of some eminent medical texts, right near "chickungunya hemorrhagic fever" and "ichthyosis."

What is the cruelest headache?

Some people get a splitting headache every time they get an orgasm. "Not tonight, dear, I have a headache" can be a self-fulfilling prophecy.

CHAPTER NINE

Interpreting DocSpeak (Hint: "Good" Means "Bad")

There are ways of delivering disagreeable news so as to make it palatable. For example, when flight attendants discuss using your seat as a flotation device, they do this in the context of a "water landing," not in the context of the plane becoming a "plummeting sarcophagus." And in the seat-back compartment in front of you, the illustrations of persons experiencing a "water landing" or an "unscheduled landing" look like this:

Jump onto slide

Salte sobre la rampa

They do not look like this:

Scream, whimper, and die

Grite, lloriquee, y muera

Every profession has its conventional euphemisms. Butchers sell "chopped sirloin," not "ground cow." Even journalism, which is supposed to be about truth telling, occasionally resorts to bull hockey. Newspapers will write about a "developing nation" even when the nation about which they are writing is not developing at all, inasmuch as it has a rooster-based economy. Euphemism is the driving force behind the classified ad:

What it says: "Cozy starter home." What it means: House is size of men's room in Exxon station.

What it says: "Attractive benefits package." What it means: Janitorial salary.

What it says: "Runs good." What it means: Owner is idiot.

The language of medicine is similarly deceptive. When doctors say a test result was "positive," that means it is bad. "Negative" test results are good. A "thrill" sounds cool, but if a doctor hears one when listening to your heart, you might keel over at any minute. An "ecchymosis" sounds revolting, but it is only a black-and-blue mark.

Among themselves, however, doctors tend to speak plainly. Surgeons will refer to a "peek-and-shriek," which is, literally, an open-and-shut case: Look in, blanch, close him up, let him die. Doctors will say a patient belongs to the Hi-Five Club, meaning he has HIV. Doctors can be real cards.

But when they are speaking in front of patients, doctors have learned the opposite skill—creative euphemism. They learn it as interns, when they are making "rounds." Rounds occur when a learned doctor in a teaching hospital goes from room to room trailed by a pack of lickspittles in lab coats who leave behind them an oily trail of sycophancy. Everyone must discuss each case in the presence of the patient. The lickspittles want to show off by exhibiting intuitive diagnostic skills, but they must do so in a manner that does not alarm the patient. They cannot say, for example, that Mr. Achenbach is "decomposing faster than a pile of fish heads in the Kalahari." They would say Mr. Achenbach is "an excellent candidate for palliative treatment" (see below).

Doctors never lose this tendency to obfuscate in front of their patients. Most people will ignore this, figuring that if there is something the doctor needs to tell you, he will get around to it in due course. Some people might even be grateful for the doctor's delicacy and diplomacy. This is not true of the hypochondriac, who is constantly looking for validation of his fears. He will assume everything the doctor says is a subterfuge to hide the ghastly truth about his condition.

Doctor: Good morning, Mr. Achenbach.
Patient: I am dying, right?
Doctor: I haven't examined you yet.
Patient: But it looks bad, doesn't it, Doc?
Doctor: We are talking on the telephone.

This sort of suspicion causes needless worry for the hypochondriac. There are only a handful of terms doctors routinely use to disguise bad things, a few dozen terms that are really, really scary but that you might not recognize. Here they are.

What They Say	What It Sounds Like	What It Means
A "mass"	A solemn religious event	Cancer
A "lesion"	A scrape	Cancer
A "mitotic process"	Some damn technical thing	Cancer
A "neoplastic involvement"	A trinket from the dollar store	Cancer
An "opacification"	Giving in to Hitler	Cancer

Yes, cancer is the leading cause of medical euphemisms; but it is not the only terrible thing that medical language is designed to hide.

What They Say	What It Sounds Like	What It Means
"AMI"	College where you can major in pig husbandry	Acute myocardial infarction, or heart attack
A "CK leak"	Calvin Klein takes a whiz	A heart attack. Refers to release of an enzyme that accompanies the death of heart muscle. Cardiologists love this term.
A "calculus"	Something hard that you want to pass	Something hard that you don't want to pass. This is a calcified stone in the gallbladder or kidney.
A "demyelinating process"	Getting salt from seawater, saving the peasants of India	Multiple sclerosis
"Secondary lues"	Reserve infielder from Dominican Republic	Syphilis, featuring crusty, weeping sores

Other medical terms are designed to hide the significance of bad symptoms.

What They Say	What It Sounds Like	What They Mean
"Exquisite"	Wonderful	Horrible. Describes pain that is incapacitating. A patient in "exquisite" pain is often whimpering and drooling.
A "bruit"	Fat guy. Beats up Popeye.	An unexpected sound when doctors listen to an organ. It is usually bad. Heart bruits, for example, can indicate CK leaks.
An "adventitious" sound	To your benefit	To your detriment. Adventitious sounds are bad lung sounds.
"Ronchi" and "stridor"	*Star Wars* characters	Specific adventitious lung sounds; they can signal anything from a cold to a tumor.
A "deficit"	A little red ink	A big red flag. A deficit means an insufficiency of something, often signaling serious illness. An "oxygen deficit" in the body is sometimes followed by coma, brain injury, a vegetative state.
A "vegetative state"	Kansas	Brain death
An "accident"	Oops. Ha ha.	Oops. Bye-bye. A grave event in your body. A cerebrovascular accident is bleeding in the brain.
"Decompensated"	Docked	Decked. It means the failure of a system–whatever ails you has reached the point that the organ in question is no longer able to maintain basic body functioning. If you have compensated liver disease, your liver is functioning well enough to sustain life. If you have decompensated liver disease, it is not.

What They Say	What It Sounds Like	What They Mean
"Discomfort"	Discomfort, as from an itch	Pain, as from insertion of a penis catheter
An "embarrassment"	A faux pas	A sudden, dramatic problem caused by an interruption to circulation or a drop in blood pressure, occasionally produced by bad diagnostic technique. Feeling for a pulse on the carotid artery on both sides of the neck at the same time, for example, can sometimes cause unconsciousness, as if the patient were being hanged. (See "syncope" below.)
A "dissection"	Something bad that happens to a frog	Something bad that happens to you. It's a spontaneous ripping and rending of tissue, as though it is being unzipped by God. When it happens to your aorta, you often die.
An "event"	A party	No party. A bad thing. A thrombotic event, for example, is a stroke.
"Iatrogenic"	A play by Aristophanes	Describes an illness or injury caused by medical treatment or diagnostic procedures. For example, sometimes a spark caused by a colonoscope will accidentally ignite intestinal gas, causing an explosion in the body. It can be fatal. And disgusting.
"Idiopathic"	Duh	Duh. When doctors diagnose an illness as idiopathic, it means they have no idea what is causing it.
An "insult"	Injured feelings	Injured flesh, often grave damage. In the autopsy report, for example, JFK's head wound was described as an "insult."

What They Say	What It Sounds Like	What They Mean
"Palliative treatment"	Some sort of treatment	No treatment. Doctors have given up on a cure. At best, they will do something final and dramatic, like amputating a gangrenous limb or creating a permanent colostomy. Usually, though, palliative treatment means doping you up until you die.
"Precocious"	Mozart	Mozart did not have huge hairy genitals at the age of four, so far as we know. Medically, a precocious development occurs unnaturally early, and is usually a very bad sign. Precocious puberty, for example, occurs in pineal hyperplasia syndrome, or tumors of the hypothalamus. Kids get adult-looking genitals at age four. No, it is not cool.
"Progressive"	Modern, forward-thinking, socially conscious	Deadly. A "progressive" disease is one that is progressing, inexorably, despite treatment. Multiple sclerosis is often described as "progressive."
"Resection"	Restore, put back, fix	Cut away. Amputate.
"Tamponade"	Women's personal hygiene procedure	Restrictive pressure on the heart, causing reduced blood flow to the body, breathlessness, and sometimes syncope.
"Syncope"	Thelonious Monk	Thelonious Monk OD's. Syncope is fainting, unconsciousness.
"Prodrome"	A dirt-floored stadium in some toilet of a town, outfitted for tractor pulls and demolition derbies	The early stage of a disease. It is often deceptively mild. Prodromal symptoms are sometimes described as "premonitory."

What They Say	What It Sounds Like	What They Mean
"Premonitory"	*You may already be a winner!*	You lose. If a symptom is premonitory, it seems trivial, but isn't. You know: Hiccups. Cancer.
A "bad result"	A bad result	A *very* bad result. This is universal DocSpeak for "death."

CHAPTER TEN

Maybe It's

Just Nerves

(Uh-Oh)

---

*O**n virtually every level,** I am unqualified to write a medical book,[1] but if simple incompetence prevented people from getting publishing contracts, John Grisham would be pushing a broom at Jiffy Lube. My ignorance is particularly overwhelming on the subject of the brain and the nervous system.

Fortunately, I had an ace in the hole: Dr. James Prokop, an eminent neurosurgeon I knew in Greenwich, Connecticut. I was counting on Dr. Prokop because of his humor and graciousness, because of his encyclopedic knowledge of his field, and because he was my wife's uncle. I was going to supply Dr. Prokop with various minor symptoms, such as eyelid twitching, and he was going to tell me how these symptoms could signify frightening neurological deterioration.[2] Privately, we would chortle over how alarmist we were being, how the human body is not so delicate a

---

1. At one point, I was planning to identify myself on the cover of this book as "Gene Weingarten, MD," revealing in very fine print that the "MD" meant that I lived in Maryland. I was persuaded not to do this by my publisher, who was concerned that it might be considered somewhat misleading, causing misunderstandings, legal actions by regulatory agencies, prison terms for all concerned, and so forth.

2. Eyelid twitching: amyotrophic lateral sclerosis, which is Lou Gehrig's disease. You waste away and then die. Also, Huntington's chorea, in which you become irritable and obnoxious, and *then* you waste away and die.

machine that sudden death awaits us all, any minute, without warning. Then, three days before I was to talk with Dr. Prokop, he suddenly died.[3]

So I am feeling a little shaky right now, trying to write about neurology. Fortunately, neurology offers the ignoramus a toehold, since much of it can be reduced to terrifying case studies and simple diagnostic exams that scare the bejesus out of you.

Reach into your pocket or purse. Feel for a quarter. Don't take it out, just explore its surfaces with your fingertips. Can you tell which side is heads and which is tails? You should be able to. This is called "stereognosis," and it is a basic test of the functioning of the parietal lobes of the brain. Failure to distinguish heads from tails can sometimes herald the presence of a parietal lobe tumor or an oncoming stroke.

Fear of strokes and brain tumors is what most frequently brings hypochondriacs to neurologists' offices. Hypochondriacs know that strokes and tumors can cause unusual symptoms, that virtually any blip or jiggle of sensation, any failure of memory, can sometimes signal something dire. My friend James Lileks, a writer who is a ferocious hypochondriac, once read that hallucinating the smell of a burnt match can mean an impending stroke. He began noticing this smell all the time, and suffering paralyzing panic attacks. It did not occur to James that the reason he was smelling burnt matches all the time was that he was lighting matches all the time. He is a cigarette smoker. This is how hypochondriacs think.

I have news for hypochondriacs. It is much *worse* than they think. Incipient strokes or tumors can create astonishing havoc in the pathways of perception, in ways hypochondriacs never would suspect, until this very moment. Yes, tumors or strokes can lead to so-called uncinate fits, which cause hallucinations of smell, but the smells are not limited to burnt phosphorus; people

---

3. Heart attack. See Chapter 11, "Infarction—Isn't That a Funny Word? Hahaha-haha Thud."

detect the odor of garbage, lemons, banana oil, wet asphalt, acrid fumes, dirty diapers. In general, perception can be wickedly distorted: A stroke victim once woke up screaming because he saw a human arm in his bed, right next to him. In fact, there *was* an arm. It was his own. He did not recognize it.

A stroke or tumor in the visual processing center of the brain can announce itself in something called the Alice in Wonderland syndrome, in which the victim sees an object and then hallucinates the same object repeatedly. Dr. Hal Blumenfeld, a neurologist I know in New Haven, Connecticut, had a patient who was looking at a potted plant in her home. A few minutes later, it reappeared. It was growing out of an omelet.

A stroke or tumor in certain areas of the cerebral cortex can make you feel as though you have been transported to a parallel universe peopled by evil impostors. This phenomenon is called "reduplicative paramnesia." You will be talking to someone who looks exactly like your brother Vincent, and sounds exactly like your brother Vincent, and still seems to have that scar from the day you launched a pushpin at him with a soupspoon, but he can't fool *you*. You are onto his little game.

A stroke or tumor in the brain's temporal lobe can result in a condition known as "jargon aphasia." The person with this condition understands what you are saying and speaks fluently in his ordinary voice, and he knows exactly what he wants to say, but the words come out all wrong. He becomes Norm Crosby, that annoying comedian who says things like "Greetings and salivations, I was expectorating you to come." No one understands the person with jargon aphasia. He is trapped in a Tower of Babel nightmare. Sometimes he commits suicide.

Parietal lobe tumors can cause a bewildering sense of spatial disorientation. You might get lost between your mailbox and your house. Or you might have difficulty putting on a shirt because you keep trying to fit your head through the armhole.

But the niftiest symptom of a stroke or brain tumor is a rare disorder called Lhermitte's peduncular hallucinosis; this was disclosed to me by Dr. Anthony Reder of the University of Chicago. Dr. Reder solemnly assured me he was not inventing this just so he could share a giggle with his graduate students by getting a preposterous fiction printed in an actual book; I assured him I did not for one minute suspect that a man of his stature and integrity would engage in such infantile behavior. Then I spent the next day searching doubtfully through neurology texts until, to my astonishment, I found it. In Lhermitte's peduncular hallucinosis, a strangling of the oxygen supply to the base of the brain causes people to see cartoonish little characters in the room, about three feet tall, often dressed in what appear to be military-type uniforms, gaily colored in pastels. They are friendly critters, completely unthreatening, and they generally go away when the cause of the oxygen deprivation is relieved, whether by drugs, surgery, or death.

Hypochondriacs do not know of these things, by and large. The symptoms of strokes and tumors that they fear are far more common: paralysis on one side of the body, muscle weakness, inability to talk. Sometimes they fear these things so desperately that they develop the symptoms, a form of hysteria. Emergency room doctors in particular are adept at weeding out the nuts, or "gomers,"[4] from the real disease victims: When a patient says he can't talk, doctors will sometimes ask him to whisper. Usually, he can. If you can whisper, then there is nothing wrong with the speech center in your brain. When a patient claims complete paralysis in an arm or appears to be unconscious, doctors will sometimes lay him on a bed, hold his hand above his face, and let go. If a patient is faking or imagining paralysis, he generally won't let his hand bash his face; it will fall to the side.

Dr. Mark Smith, director of the Washington Hospital Center emergency room in Washington, D.C., once confronted a patient who complained of paralysis on the right side of his body. Indeed, the right side appeared to be flaccid, but Smith was sus-

---

4. **G**et **O**ut of **M**y **E**mergency **R**oom.

picious. So he asked the person to make a series of voluntary motions with the right side of his body. Nothing. Finally, Dr. Smith asked him to turn his head to the left and right. He could turn it to the left, but not to the right. Bingo. Turning to the right is accomplished by a muscle on the left side of the neck, and vice versa.

Tumors and strokes. Strokes and tumors. The basic, boring repertoire of the hypochondriac. And then suddenly, a few years ago, some neurologists found themselves facing a new complaint. The disease was actually an old one, identified in 1920. But no one had heard about it until cows in England started behaving in an uncivil manner, which greatly distressed the Brits, who wear formal attire to cockfights. This was, of course, the debut of "mad cow disease." If you eat the meat of an infected animal, it can cause a fatal nerve disorder known as Creutzfeldt-Jakob disease. By all rights none of this should have caused much consternation in the United States because

1. These were British cows.
2. No one outside England seemed to be sick.
3. Globally, Creutzfeldt-Jakob disease is a one-in-a-million occurrence, mostly seen in tissue-transplant patients, so rare that as an epidemic it had previously been sighted only in the 1950s in the eastern highlands of Papua New Guinea, in the form of a fatal illness called kuru. Kuru was eradicated when the residents of the eastern highlands of Papua New Guinea were persuaded to stop eating one another.

Unfortunately, this triad was not enough to allay the fears of American hypochondriacs, because the symptoms of Creutzfeldt-Jakob disease are dismayingly familiar. The disease causes you to get nervous and twitchy and tired, and leads to a "spongiform brain," in which your brain tissue literally gets soft and squishy and your ability to think and remember deteriorates rapidly. Who among us has not from time to time, particularly on Sunday mornings, suspected himself of having a spongiform brain? The Internet filled up with terrified postings from hypochondriacs, including one highly literate woman who said her life had become a hellish cycle of unfounded medical fears: "When I forget a name or a telephone number, I feel that panicked realization that my brain is already sponging up and will soon have the consistency of a Nerf ball."

It is not that hypochondriacs *want* to be sick, but the fact is there are certain diseases that are irresistible to them, diseases that mimic the sorts of symptoms caused by the stresses of modern life and the ravages of age. This gives them something to help explain why they are so damned tired and achy all the time and why things seem to slip from their minds. They want an explanation other than that they are getting old and forgetful and their bodies are inexorably breaking down and life from that point on will be a graceless descent into senescence and groaning decrepitude. They want to blame it on a bug. The degree of fear and excitement exhibited by hypochondriacs is proportional to the severity of the disease they suspect, and in the case of mad cow disease, an inevitably fatal condition, the steaks were high.[5]

In time, the furor waned. And then, bang, it was back. In September 1997, University of Kentucky scientists reported five cases of Creutzfeldt-Jakob disease linked to the consumption of scrambled eggs with squirrel brains, which apparently is something of a delicacy among gap-toothed hillbillies in bib overalls who live in towns with names like West Horse Jowl, Kentucky. This brought the hypochondriacs out again.

This is, of course, ridiculous. Normal people don't eat squirrel brains. Normal people are much more likely to get bitten by a tick and get Lyme disease, which causes you to feel tired and achy and forgetful. Hypochondriacs love Lyme disease; internists probably diagnose one or two cases of Lyme disease a year, but they deal with dozens of people who think they have it and seem mildly disappointed to learn they do not.

Lyme disease causes peripheral neuropathies, which are debilitating disorders affecting muscles and the nerves that control them. Eventually, peripheral neuropathies can make the skin feel as though you are wearing stockings and gloves all the time.

---

5. Get it?

Earlier, it is subtler. It can be detected by a basic diagnostic pro-cedure called "two-point-discrimination tests."

Get two pins, and a ruler with millimeter markings. Touch the skin in various parts of the body with the two pins held apart at varying dis-tances to see how close together the points must be before you feel the stimulus as a single point, not two. Different parts of the body should have different degrees of sensitivity, and, no, the fingertips are only the *second* most sensitive organ. First are the lips and tongue, a rather nice piece of work by the Almighty, who, after all, puts great em-phasis on the perpetuation of the species, if you get my meaning. In general, the lips and the tongue should be able to discriminate be-tween points that are 1 millimeter apart. Next, the fingertips: 2 to 8 mil-limeters. The toes: 3 to 8 millimeters. The palm of the hand: 8 to 12. The chest and forearms: 40. The back: 40 to 70. The upper arms and thighs: 75. Keep experimenting with distances. In these normal ranges, if you consistently feel two pinpricks as one, you might have peripheral neuropathy. Not a good thing to have. This could be evi-dence not only of Lyme disease but of any number of other serious conditions, including diabetes, AIDS, and poisoning by arsenic or cyanide. Impaired two-point discrimination can also signal damage to the spinal cord typical of multiple sclerosis.

Still unsure? Take off your shoes and socks. Have someone take a small bluntly pointed object, like a swizzle stick, and scrape it lightly down the sole of your foot, from the heel to the base of the little toe, and then across to the ball of the foot. Your toes should clench, which is called the plantar reflex. If they don't, it could indicate peripheral neu-ropathies. Sometimes you get an opposite reaction, in which the toes extend upward and the big toe fans out. This is called a positive Babin-ski sign, and it is often bad news. It suggests some disease or break-down in the motor pathways of the central nervous system.

Other simple tests can detect basic neurological problems:

Lie on your back. Take the heel of one foot and place it on the opposite knee. Run the heel down the center of the leg, staying on the shinbone. This is called the heel-shin test, and it is a surprisingly sensitive way to detect early disease of the cerebellum, the portion of the brain that controls equilibrium and voluntary muscular activity. Your heel should be able to stay to the middle of the leg without deviating to the sides or showing hesitant, herky-jerky motion. Cerebellar disease eventually may result in an unsteady gait and, ultimately, inability to walk. Among the conditions that sometimes can be diagnosed with this test is . . . Creutzfeldt-Jakob disease!

Sit on the edge of a bed or table that lets your legs swing free. Have a friend take a small hammer and tap you lightly but sharply on the knee, about a half inch below the lower edge of the kneecap. This is, of course, the famous patellar reflex. Most people think that if there is a muscle reaction, it is good. That is not necessarily so. Your foot should swing forward, but just a little. A very strong reaction—say, if you kick your friend's teeth in—is not good; it suggests some lesion in the brain or spinal cord. No reaction at all suggests that you are a professional ballet dancer who goes on pointe, or that you have peripheral neuropathies, or, most likely, that you did the test wrong. And an opposite reaction—the foot swings backward—is symptomatic of a tumor or other injury to the lumbar portion of the spinal cord.

One last test. This will seem familiar. Go to a mirror, put a Popsicle stick in your mouth, press down on your tongue, and say "ahh." You probably thought doctors did this to inspect your tonsils. Sometimes they are checking for the proper operation of your cranial nerves.[6] Your uvula is supposed to rise a little, and vibrate, but remain in the center

---

6. In medical school, students learn an ancient mnemonic device to remember the names of the twelve cranial nerves: "On old Olympus's towering tops, a Finn and German viewed a hops" (olfactory, optic, oculomotor, trochlear, etc.). Because this basically makes no sense at all, in recent years smart-ass male medical students corrupted it to "Oh, oh, oh, to touch and feel a girl's vagina and hymen!"—which, not surprisingly, has stuck. Some of these male medical students have gone on to become pillars of their communities. In general, medical books love mnemonic devices. The best one I found summarizes the causes of urinary incontinence: **D**ehydration, **R**etention, **I**nfection, **P**sychologic.

of the throat. If it moves to one side or the other, it suggests a disorder involving the vagus or glossopharyngeal nerves. This can indicate a brain tumor or a stroke.

And now, some important commonly asked scientific questions about the brain and central nervous system.

During the Reign of Terror, when someone was guillotined and his head plopped off into a wicker basket, and some French revolutionary, drunk on power and revenge, held the head up by the hair in front of a ravening crowd of semiliterate bloodthirsty keening yeehaws with bad teeth, might there have been a few horrifying seconds when the head was still conscious and saw this happen?

Yes. In 1988, scientists published the results of a study called *Neocortical and Hippocampal Electrical Activity Following Decapitation in Rats,* in which persons in white lab coats with advanced degrees took a bunch of rats and chopped their heads off. Then they measured the severed brains for the persistence of electrical impulses suggesting consciousness. Electrical activity continued for thirteen to fourteen seconds after decapitation. This is long enough to hum the first eight bars of "La Marseillaise."

What's the story with that slashing karate chop to the back of the neck that lets the hero temporarily incapacitate the villain in old TV shows like the original Mission: Impossible? *And wasn't Peter Lupus the worst actor of all time?*

The unconsciousness-inducing karate chop is a clumsy plot device to effectuate sudden, improbable escapes. It would not work in real life; neurologists say a vicious blow to the back of the neck could conceivably cause paralysis but probably not unconsciousness, unless it also killed you. Peter Lupus is the third-worst actor of all time, after Victor Mature and the guy who played the Professor on *Gilligan's Island.* The worst acting *performance* of all time was by Shelley Duvall in *The Shining.*

Is there any neurological disease that can turn you into a sex machine? How do I get it?

Herpes simplex encephalitis is a serious infection that can attack the temporal lobes of the brain. With proper treatment you can recover, though sometimes there is irreversible damage done to the brain tissue, and permanent memory loss. One rare but possible complication from herpes simplex encephalitis is Kluver-Bucy syndrome, in which you become "hyperoral." You try to put everything in your mouth. You show symptoms of pica, which is a desire to eat bizarre things, such as dirt or hair or cigarettes. You also have indiscriminate sexual urges. You become a voracious, sex-crazed, humping lunatic. Cats with Kluver-Bucy syndrome will rape chickens. Humans get wildly horny. They suck and lick at your face. They squeeze and probe your body. They rub their privates against you. They have no idea that there is anything wrong with this.

Shouldn't a book on hypochondria deal with psychiatric disorders?

It should. Except psychiatry is in disorganized retreat these days, with mounting evidence that the hallowed tenets and principles of psychotherapy, long considered the glorious apex of modern medical achievement, are about as valid as the theory that the earth sits on a big turtle. Sigmund Freud, the brilliant brainmaster who became the model for a thousand fictional shrinks with ludicrous Teutonic accents, is now widely regarded as Daffy the Quack. People who spent twenty years weeping out their family secrets to psychotherapists are now cured by a pill. Psychotherapists are going to work for Wal-Mart, leaving behind a pile of grease-stained inkblots.

Are Rorschach tests discredited, too?

Not really. They remain a reasonably reliable diagnostic tool to identify delusional or pathological thinking. The key is that the blots themselves are randomly generated and therefore meaningless. The patient must supply the interpretation, drawing from within; most of us offer benign scenarios. It is here that pathologies sometimes reveal themselves. On the following page is a typical set of random Rorschach blots. Try it yourself.

CHAPTER ELEVEN

Infarction—Isn't That a Funny Word? Hahahahaha Thud.

S he was the kind of dame who gets your attention if you are the kind of guy who doesn't know the difference between ecru and puce, if you get my drift. She was brainy but not mouthy. She walked fast but fine, like a woman who knows how a woman is supposed to walk but doesn't give a damn. Not that she walked like a man. A goat can't impersonate a fish.

She took my hands in hers. Her hands felt good. Mine felt clammy, like a clam. That's the thing about me. When I'm nervous, I can't think of good analogies. She took the tips of my fingers in hers and pressed on them, not enough to hurt but enough to let me know she could hurt me if she wanted to. She had hurt men, you could tell.

We were alone in a small room with a bed. I took off my tie. I took off my shirt. She reached for me. We had sex.

OK, we didn't have sex, because Dr. Karen Stark is a cardiologist and it would have been totally inappropriate for us to have sex in her office, plus I was wearing one of those paper gowns that expose your behind, and I am certain Dr. Stark would have been laughing too hard to properly enjoy the experience.

I was in her Washington office to get my heart listened to. I didn't have a heart problem, so far as I knew. In twenty years of active, aggressive hypochondria, my heart was the only organ that I never once suspected of betraying me. When I decided to get a medical exam as part of my research, I chose a cardiologist, because I felt reasonably secure. So here I was in Dr. Stark's office, practically *daring* her to find something wrong.

She put a stethoscope on my chest. She frowned. She listened again. She said: "You have an extra heart—"

I knew it! Suddenly, all became clear: The racing pulse in times of stress! The pounding in my ears when I climbed that pyramid in Mexico! I had an extra heart! But wait. Was this good, or bad? Maybe it is like having a dual carburetor or, holy cow, a second penis. You could be a superman, the *Übermensch* Nietzsche dreamed of. But what if . . .

"—beat."

"Pardon me?"

"You have an extra heartbeat. Everyone has a few extra heartbeats."

"Oh. So it is no problem?"

"Right," she said.

But she wasn't really listening. Sometimes you can tell that with a woman, particularly if she has a stethoscope on your chest and she is saying "shhh."

"Squat down," she commanded.

(Oboy.)

"You have a midsystolic click," Dr. Stark said at last, pleased. I had asked her to find something wrong, and she did. It is called a mitral valve prolapse. Basically, the valve between my left atrium and left ventricle is a little squishy, and when it opens and contracts, part of it squeegies through the hole and makes a click, and a lot of people have it; it is sort of a benign hernia[1] of the heart, and there is probably nothing to worry about, and

---

1. By the way, during a hernia exam, when a doctor says, "Turn your head and cough," did you ever wonder why you had to turn your head? Is that somehow part of the incredibly sensitive musculovisceral response that he is feeling with his educated fingers in your groin? One day I asked the doctor why you have to turn your head. He explained: "So you do not cough on *me*."

there is certainly no reason to run home and throw open your two hundred medical books and read everything ever written about valves, including Chilton automotive manuals.

According to *The Cecil Textbook of Medicine* (twentieth edition), a mitral valve prolapse is no big deal, except for the possible development of infectious endocarditis, which is basically a rampaging infection of the heart that deposits what is known, euphemistically, as "vegetation" inside the organ and can kill you. But—and this is a big but[2]—"if ventricular irritability is present, the extent of the murmur of hypertrophic cardiomyopathy with obstruction is much louder in the post extrasystolic beat." I have no idea what this means, but it doesn't sound good. Fortunately, at this point my attention was distracted by a picture of a woman who has no thumb as a result of congenital heart disease. A problem with the heart can make your thumb fall off!

I have to stop reading these books.

A few days after my chest exam, I was leafing through a health magazine, noticing endless lists of support groups for persons with, shall we say, cutting-edge medical conditions. There were support groups for victims of anxiety disorders and eating disorders and "pet grief" and attention deficit disorders and obsessive-compulsive obsessive-compulsive obsessive-compulsive disorders, and something called "trichotillomania," which is defined as chronic hair pulling. And there in the middle of these listings was a support group for victims of . . . mitral valve prolapse! So I called the phone number that was listed and I told the woman who answered that I had a mitral valve prolapse, and she said—and I am quoting here—"I'm so sorry." I said the cardiologist told me it was nothing to worry about, and there was a full five seconds of pregnant, patronizing silence. Finally, she spoke.

"I faint all the time," she said.

See, that's the problem for hypochondriacs. Sometimes you

---

2. Speaking of which, there is a medical condition called "bitrochanteric lipodystrophy" in which most of the fat in your body is concentrated in your thighs and buttocks, which get grotesquely enlarged. The downside of this condition is that you waddle like a platypus and scare the neighborhood dogs. The upside is that on Halloween you can wrap yourself in aluminum foil, stick some toilet paper in your collar, and you make a *fabulous* Hershey's® Kiss.

just don't know whom to believe—a qualified professional like Dr. Stark or some anonymous whack job on the telephone. Fortunately, at that point I had already been cured of my hypochondria in a miracle of modern science that I will disclose a few chapters from now. So I felt faint only for a few minutes, and then it passed.

Although cardiologists have an arsenal of sophisticated tests, such as echocardiograms, many initial diagnoses are made simply by listening to your chest, taking your blood pressure, observing your breathing, evaluating your skin tone, checking whether you have any thumbs, etc. And so it is that you can sometimes play cardiologist in your own bathroom, without the formality of eight years of higher education, sucking up to professors, gobbling amphetamines like Tic Tacs, and so forth.

 Quick! Go to a mirror. Check out your earlobe. Is it creased? There is a surprising correlation between persons with a crease going at least halfway across their earlobes diagonally and persons who have, or are likely to develop, coronary artery disease. Coronary artery disease is not good. "Coronary artery disease" has been the leading cause of death ever since it overtook "being eaten by wildebeest." True fact: Surviving statuary of the Roman emperor Hadrian, believed to have died of heart disease, shows just such an earlobe crease.

The earlobe crease is a highly unsophisticated sign, though. A far more reliable indication of heart disease is "clubbing," an abnormal enlargement of the fingertips. That is one of the reasons Dr. Stark was pressing my fingernails—she was checking out the nail bed. Of course, she knew what she was looking for, and you do not. Fortunately for you, there is a simple test for clubbing, called the Schamroth procedure.

Take the middle fingers of both hands and extend them, as though you were making a rude gesture toward this book. (You can stop now.)

Now place the two fingers together, parallel, back to back, knuckle touching knuckle, nail touching nail, with your right hand to the left of your left hand. (You will have to cross your forearms to do this.) Inspect the small area between the nail beds. There should be a space there, roughly the shape of an elongated diamond, or a rhombus, approximately two millimeters wide at its widest point. Got it? No? If there is no space, you may have clubbing, which can indicate any number of serious cardiopulmonary diseases, including bronchiectasis (which is an often irreversible destructive disease of the bronchial walls), or endocarditis (which is a potentially fatal inflammation of the lining of the heart), or even lung cancer (which needs no introduction). It also might mean nothing is wrong with your heart: You might have liver disease, or esophageal cancer.

Now take your pulse, at the wrist. Then count your heartbeats for the same number of seconds. Now do it again. And again. If your pulse is consistently slower than your heartbeat, this is a condition known as a "pulse deficit." It is an indication of heart arrhythmia. Heart arrhythmia can be benign, but it can also mean heart disease, particularly in the left ventricle, which is the main pumping chamber. To be significant, a pulse deficit would have to be constant. You would have to test yourself again and again. And again. Day and night, until you were sure. Which is ridiculous. You're probably fine. Check it again, why don't you?

If you are getting confused, don't feel bad. The heart is highly complex; there are many confusing things about it. For example, did you ever wonder why the human heart is represented this way in Valentine's Day cards?

The answer is that it would look ridiculous this way:

The fact is, the human heart and lungs are nauseating-looking organs. They swell and shrink and thump and pulse. They are filigreed with angry purple blood vessels and operate beneath membranes that are about as attractive as that slimy thing that covers your dog's open eyeball when he's asleep. If a spaceship landed on earth and out stepped an alien that looked exactly like a human heart and lungs, the townspeople would kill it with pitchforks. But fortunately, we do not have to look at these organs. Inside our body, they work together, medically inseparable, astonishingly efficient, to keep us alive. So, breathe easier. If you can.

 Breathe normally and count the number of in-out breaths you take in one minute. Normal respiration is 12 to 20 per minute. Now take your pulse. The ratio of respirations to heartbeats should be approximately 1 to 4. If you are breathing more rapidly than that, it can simply mean you are showing anxiety over this test. And well you might: Sustained fast breathing, known as "tachypnea," can indicate cardiac insufficiency, emphysema, thyroid disease, metabolic disease, and sometimes tumors in the brain stem. Unusually *low* breathing rates, known as "bradypnea," sometimes can signal illnesses not directly related to the lungs: incipient kidney failure, strokes or tumors in the cerebrum, or even myasthenia gravis, a debilitating neuromuscular disease that can turn you into a human beanbag chair.

 Take a deep breath, and then start counting rapidly out loud. If your lungs are functioning normally, you should be able to count to 70 or so before you need to take a breath. If you don't get near that, your lungs may be showing diminished volume, which could indicate restrictive lung disease. This would be anything that makes it hard to take deep, full breaths, including an array of lung diseases and infections ranging from pneumonia to lung cancer to kyphoscoliosis, a malformation of the spine sometimes associated with heart disease.

 Breathe normally. Time your inhalations and exhalations. In general, each exhaled breath should take about twice as long from start to finish as each inhaled breath. If it takes significantly longer, it is a sign of obstructive lung disease, which is anything that makes it hard to breathe out, such as asthma, bronchiectasis, bronchitis, or emphysema.

 Stand up. Hold both arms straight above your head, with the sides of your arms touching your ears. Remain in that position for three minutes. If you feel stuffiness, or nasal congestion, or dizziness, this is called Pemberton's sign, and it can mean you have thyroid disease or an obstruction in the large veins leading to the heart—possibly a blood clot or tumor.

Place your index finger next to the shinbone about halfway between the knee and the ankle. Press in for several seconds, and release. The skin should very briefly dimple inward, but return to its normal state almost immediately. A dimple that lasts more than a second or two may be a problem. This is called edema, a fluid buildup in the tissues that can signal heart or lung disorders. A dimple that lasts a minute or more may indicate impending failure of the right side of the heart.

If you are like most people, your principal fear is a heart attack, or an "acute myocardial infarction." This occurs when blood flow to the heart is interrupted, and it can result in the death of heart muscle. In recent years, the risk of heart attacks has been reduced by various medical techniques, including angioplasty, a procedure in which coronary arteries, blocked by a buildup of cholesterol from years of eating things like ham hocks and Mallomars, are snaked out with an instrument that is, basically, a $500,000 pipe cleaner. This is a somewhat controversial procedure inasmuch as it has been known to cause certain complications, such as death.

Death does not faze cardiologists, however. Cardiologists have embraced risk taking ever since South African surgeon Christiaan Barnard first transplanted a human heart, in 1967, in an operation that brought him fame, riches, and everlasting acclaim even though the patient died blue and gasping a few days later. Cardiologists' resultant gung ho mentality has led to many medical breakthroughs in the last thirty years, the most dramatic of which is the development of a procedure called coronary bypass, in which blood flow is diverted from a diseased coronary artery to a healthy blood vessel grafted from elsewhere in the body. Twenty years ago this was considered a dangerous surgery. But techniques rapidly improved. People began getting "double bypasses," involving two blood vessels, and then "triple" and "quadruple" bypasses, with surgeons competing for greater numbers of bypassed vessels until they ran out of mathematical terminology and had to start making up names, like "super-squintiple" bypass.

Doctors are still experimenting. The big news in the heart business these days is a Brazilian surgeon named Randas Batista, who is becoming the darling of the medical world. He treats people with congestive heart failure by gouging out huge hunks of their hearts, which he keeps in his office in jelly jars. He is considered a genius.

Everyone knows the classic symptoms of a heart attack: pain below the sternum in the center of the chest, sometimes radiating to the neck or jaw or down the inside surface of the left arm, often accompanied by nausea and difficulty breathing. Many people think that those symptoms pretty much sum up the worrisome type of chest pain. Ha ha. Many people are nitwits. Significant chest pains come in many subtle variations, like fine cheeses. The thing to remember about chest pains is that on the surface they may seem as different as Velveeta and Brie, yet, by and large, in the end, they all indicate that something, somewhere, has rotted.

If the pain seems like a tightness in a band across the chest, and if it gets worse with exertion, emotion, or eating, it might be angina pectoris, known as ischemic heart disease. This is caused by blocked coronary vessels that don't permit sufficient blood flow to the heart. If the pain is steady and oppressive and hurts more when you are lying down or breathing deeply, and less if you are leaning forward, it could be pericarditis. This is a potentially life-threatening inflammation of the membrane covering the heart, which can be caused by infection or tumor or even an oncoming heart attack. If the pain is deep and crushing, with nausea, weakness, and extreme shortness of breath, it could be an embolism in the pulmonary artery, or some other serious interruption of blood flow to the lungs. If the pain is sudden and nearly disabling, feeling as though your chest is being torn open from the inside, that could be a rupturing aortic aneurysm, which basically means your chest is being torn open from the inside. Usually, you die.

But often, minor chest pains mean nothing. Doctors are forever trying to tell that to the hypochondriac, without much success. A case in point is the true story of Heart Attack Holmes, a man who became famous among the young residents at the George Washington University Medical Center emergency room in the late 1970s.

Mr. Holmes was a polite man who would come in practically every weekend complaining that he was having a heart attack. He described the pain with medical precision. Each time, doctors would check him out. Each time, he was perfectly healthy.

Heart Attack Holmes was a big joke among the smart young doctors at George Washington University Medical Center. Tending to him became something of a rite of passage. He was the classic hypochondriac.

One Saturday, Heart Attack Holmes came into the emergency room and said he was having a heart attack.

And he was. Dropped dead, right on the spot.

CHAPTER TWELVE

Are You

an

Alcoholic?

———————

Nearly two-thirds of Americans drink alcoholic beverages, and in this health-conscious age, many of them are worried that their consumption is excessive. Studies keep suggesting that excessive drinking increases the risk of several diseases, including anemia, pancreatic cancer, oral cancer, esophageal cancer, and osteoporosis. At the same time, studies keep suggesting also that moderate intake of alcohol can actually be beneficial, lowering blood pressure, reducing cholesterol levels, preventing heart disease.

It's all very confusing. How much drinking is moderate? How much is too much? What distinguishes the normal drinker from the problem drinker? Organizations like Alcoholics Anonymous have created simple diagnostic checklists to gauge whether your drinking makes you an alcoholic. Unfortunately, asking Alcoholics Anonymous if you need Alcoholics Anonymous is like asking your kid if you need a puppy. AA's tests have a very low threshold. A typical quiz from Alcoholics Anonymous asks questions like these:

1. Do you sometimes feel "tipsy" after drinking?
2. Have you ever inadvertently consumed more alcohol than you intended to?
3. Do you ever drink alone?
4. Do people ever criticize you for your drinking?
5. Have you ever woken up with a headache from excessive drinking the night before?

And so forth.

You take the test and are fairly proud that you have answered "no" to most of the biggies. So you sit down to grade yourself and discover that a single "yes" answer means you are in danger of becoming an alcoholic. Two "yes" answers mean you *are* an alcoholic!

The average hypochondriac will at this point be in a blind panic; he will look up the signs of alcoholism in his extensive medical library and learn that the alcoholic has "increased mean corpuscular volume, increased gamma-glutamyltransferase, increased aspartate amino transferase, and increased low-density lipoprotein cholesterol." He will have no idea what any of these things mean, but he will worry about them obsessively. He will suspect in himself the dreaded "beer potomania," observed in people who drink more than eight quarts of beer a day, a condition in which you have too much water in your blood and do not pee enough, which causes "water intoxication," which can lead to confusion and lethargy and death. He will realize he has exhibited signs of neurological weaknesses typical of alcoholics, which can include twitches that are very, very shockingly like the eyelid twitches he has been increasingly noticing since the first chapter of this book. He will strongly suspect Wernicke-Korsakoff syndrome, in which alcohol poisoning leads to a lack of thiamine in the blood, causing hemorrhagic lesions in the brain, impairing the loss of the ability to encode new information or remember recent events. He will not rule out Marchiafava-Bignami disease, which is an alcohol-induced decay of the corpus callosum, at the center of the brain, first detected in chronic drinkers of red wine in Italy, causing a clumsy gait, followed by stupor and seizures.

He will not go to the doctor, because all of this is way too embarrassing, but he will relentlessly monitor himself for signs of neurological deterioration. To prove to himself that he is coordinated, he will, for the first time in his life, get out on a dance floor, where he will resemble a camel attempting to goose-step. He will constantly be checking his mental acuity, going up to total strangers in the street and saying, "It is Monday, the third of March, which is, by my calculation, the sixty-second day of the year 1997 and my mother's maiden name was Frelinghuysen." He will contrive to attend parties in which doctors will be in attendance so he can drop lines like, "So, I was just wondering whether a runny nose might indicate excessive gamma-glutamyltransferase in the blood."

The hypochondriac will, in fact, tear himself apart, even though his drinking typically consists of a Pabst at dinner.

I contend this worry is in itself unhealthy. I contend we need to update the drinking test to weed out the healthy, normal drinker from the genuine alcoholic and to redirect the hypochondriac to more productive worries, such as whether that occasional stabbing pain up the rectum, the one that stops all conversation, might be cancer.[1]

Here's a new test:

ARE YOU AN ALCOHOLIC?

1. Have you ever felt guilty about your drinking? Did another drink help?
2. Do you ever drink alone? Are you drinking alone right now? Directly from the bottle? Standing naked in the shower in case you vomit?
3. Do people sometimes criticize you for your drinking? When you attempt to punch them in the face, do you fall down?
4. When you drive drunk, are you generally sober enough to keep one eye closed so your vision is not double? Good for you.

---

1. Sure it might!

5. Have you ever eaten the worm and then discovered that it was not, in fact, the worm, but something else wormlike that happened to be in the vicinity of the bottle, for example, an egg sac from a cockroach?

6. Have you ever awakened in an intensive care unit, with uniformed police officers standing over you, arguing with doctors who were saying you could not be questioned until you were "out of the woods"?

7. Are you ever slightly embarrassed to discover you have one alcoholic beverage in your hand, another on the table, and a third in a hypodermic syringe that you are about to inject directly into your stomach, for a better "rush"?

8. Do you sometimes find that you have been made the butt of a sucker bet among your friends, such as whether you will actually drink from the toilet with a Flavor Straw for a quarter?

9. At times when no alcohol was available, have you ever consumed other substances because you thought they might contain alcohol, such as naphtha or Massengill Sta-Fresh douche?

10. Have you ever urinated into an empty beer can to avoid having to negotiate your way to the bathroom, and then forgotten you had done this, and . . . you know? Has this ever happened more than once in the same night? Do you think it might have ever happened and you did not notice?

GRADING

You are not an alcoholic.

CHAPTER THIRTEEN

Tumor.
Rhymes with
"Humor."

This book is breathtakingly free of serious research, but I did interview a few dozen doctors. Each time, I would smile engagingly and explain that I was writing a humorous book about fatal diseases. The doctor's expression would not change. If you are a doctor you must be adroit at hiding your reactions. A patient must feel the doctor is taking him seriously when he complains, for example, that he gets an erection every time he sneezes. So each doctor I was interviewing would hear me out stone faced and pray that someone would begin to hemorrhage in his waiting room so he had an excuse to bolt and run.

Interviews with oncologists were the hardest. Oncologists are grave. Their offices are grim places. While I was explaining to one of them the terrific ironic potential in disease, patients in the next room were undergoing infusions of poison. Eventually, as I got to the part about the delicate synergy between comedy and tragedy, the doctor said: "Fifty percent of my patients are dead within five years of their first appointment."

Ah, I said.

I tried to lighten the mood. I observed that this 50 percent figure must be frustrating. It would be like being a lawyer who defends only skinhead homicidal maniacs whose crimes were witnessed by archbishops with video cameras.

"I have to tell people they are going to die," the doctor said.

The interview was not going well.

"So, um, how do they react when you tell them they are going to die?"

"Badly. They get very upset."

Ah.

I tried to think of something positive: "Is there any part of the human body that cancer cannot reach? Any organ, any body part, in which you cannot get a tumor?"

Evidently, no one had asked him this before. A quarter century of experience rolled through his brain. Cancer in bone, blood, muscle, skin, gristle. Cancers of the tongue, the pineal gland, the uvula, the tonsil, the penis. Cancers of the scrotum, the eyelid, the armpit, the scalp. Cancers of the ear, the elbow, the anus, the belly button. He shook his head doubtfully.

"The appendix?" I prompted.

"You can get cancer there."

"The finger?"

"Yep. Big one, right under the nail."

"The nipple?"

He looked at me like I was a protozoan. "That is breast cancer."

Ah, right.

At last, he thought of one. "The lens of the eye!" he said.

That's *it*?

"I *think* you can't get a tumor there. Never seen one. Doesn't mean it can't happen."

He excused himself. He had work to do. Death awaited.

I left his office depressed. I had begun to give up on finding humor in cancer when I walked into the Washington office of Dr. Henry Fox, oncologist. On that very day, Eric Davis, star outfielder for the Baltimore Orioles, had been diagnosed with a tumor in the colon. Inevitably, the media had described it as "the size of a baseball."[1]

"Lucky he isn't a basketball player," said Dr. Fox.

---

1. Thus violating the ancient newspaper convention that all tumors must be compared in size to fruits and vegetables. I am hoping this is the start of a new era of creativity in tumor comparison. Just once I would like to see a doctor describe a tumor as "the size of a cheese blintz."

A glimmer of hope.

So, Doctor, what's funny about cancer?

He brightened. "I actually have a file here on humor some-where," he said. He rummaged in his bookcase and found it. It was as thin as a potato chip. A single newspaper clipping flut-tered out. It was by me.

He put the file back on the shelf.

"Let's see," he said. "Humor. OK, what is the difference be-tween Sloan-Kettering and Shea Stadium?"

Dunno, I said.

"At Sloan-Kettering, the mets always win."

Ha ha, I said. What?

"See, 'mets' is an abbreviation for 'metastasis,' which is a cancer that has spread systemically from one organ or system to another."

Ah.

A desperate silence filled the room.

"Actually," Dr. Fox said, "I guess there is not much funny about cancer."

Oncologists routinely get patients who have noticed a lump and are terrified. My hypochondriac friend James Lileks follows a basic diagnostic procedure when he discovers a hard mass that didn't seem to be there the day before. Knowing that the human body is bilaterally symmetric, he feels to see if there is a corre-sponding lump on the other side of the body. Only if there isn't does he get alarmed.

I told this to Dr. Fox, to illustrate the medical principle that James Lileks is a moron.

"Actually," he said, "that will work most of the time."

Like all oncologists, Dr. Fox has hypochondriac patients. "I only have a few," he says, "but I see them often."

It turns out many hypochondriacs have figured out the Lileks Rule. But that doesn't help: A test of symmetry does not screen out most of the harmless lumps that will bring people to oncolo-gists' offices. In increasing order of frequency, here are the four leading stupid causes of concern among the lumpin' proletariat:

4. *The xiphoid process:* This is the bony prominence at the bottom of the breastbone. Everybody has one. Only one. Every oncologist has had to tell somebody, sometime, that the terrifying lump he has found is as normal as a nose.

3. *The epididymis:* This is a long, gnarled tube that carries sperm from the testicle to the penis.[2] It arches near the top of the testicle, where it can feel hard and wormy; typically, one side feels lumpier than the other. It can feel like a third testicle. No one wants a third testicle.[3]

2. *Zits:* Particularly, those creepy painful gouty lumps in the earlobe.

1. *The inframammary ridge:* This is a firm line of compressed tissue along the lower edge of every woman's breast, near the ribs. Even some doctors mistake it for a mass.

In an uncharacteristic exercise of good taste and judgment, I am not going to say much more about breast lumps in women. This is because I don't want to write anything that might dissuade a woman from seeing a doctor if she finds a lump. Lives are saved by early diagnosis. See your doctor, ladies. Your only risk is that he is going to have to sit you down and patiently explain to you that different breasts have different textures and consistencies—that some (like Cindy Crawford's) feel smooth and soft and creamy, like a baby's bottom, while others (like

---

2. The epididymis feels like "a knotted strand of al dente spaghetti," according to *The Art and Science of Bedside Diagnosis,* a colorful, highly eccentric text for doctors that relentlessly compares body parts to food. For the record, the testicle "feels like a hard-boiled pigeon's egg."

3. James Lileks contends that God placed the testicles on the outside of the body specifically to torment hypochondriacs. He points out that if one is a man, one's testicles are particularly unsettling terrain: They are the only actual internal bodily organs that are right out there in the open. You can inventory the lumps, even in the privacy of your own pants. Apparently having no sense of personal dignity whatsoever, James happily discussed this for publication. He observes that if it were possible to extrude your pancreas from your navel and examine it for lumps, hypochondriacs would be examining their pancreases forty times a day. With their testicles, they can do this, so they do.

yours) feel like a Hefty garbage bag filled with human molars and minestrone soup.

Wherever they occur, lumps are undeniably scary. There are no hard rules for diagnosing which are cancerous and which are not, but there are some general guidelines:

1. Pain is good. Cancerous tumors generally do not hurt.
2. Heat is good. A lump that is warm to the touch probably is an infection, not cancer.
3. Pus is good. You usually can't express liquid from a cancerous tumor.
4. Change is good. A cancerous tumor will seldom wax and wane in size. It will steadily grow.
5. Soft is good. Cancerous tumors tend to be hard.

If a hypochondriac has no lumps to worry about, he will look for moles. Moles could be malignant melanomas, some of the deadliest cancers around. They are a hypochondriac's delight. This is because malignant melanomas are nearly 100 percent curable if caught early enough, and nearly 100 percent deadly if not caught early enough. This encourages obsessive vigilance. Dermatologists get a lot of hypochondriac traffic.

Concerned if your mole is malignant?

1. Solid color is good. Melanomas tend to be multicolored, often with patriotic tinges of red, white, or blue.
2. Small is good. Melanomas tend to be at least the diameter of a pencil eraser.
3. Symmetrical is good. Melanomas tend to have ragged edges and oddball shapes.
4. Hairy is good. Melanomas tend to be bald.
5. Boring is good. Melanomas sometimes change their appearance from week to week.
6. Dry is good. Melanomas sometimes bleed.
7. Smooth is good. Melanomas sometimes ulcerate and have a crusty texture. They can crumble to the touch.

Note to hypochondriacs: You might want to clip out the previous two lists. Good. Now flush them down the toilet. They are unreliable. Cancerous tumors are outlaws. Rebels. They don't always follow the rules. To use a medical analogy, if the human body were Thomas W. Pyle Middle School in Bethesda, Maryland, and lumps and moles were the students of Mrs. Schlom's eighth-grade science class, then a malignant tumor would be my son, Dan, who cut class, set a roll of toilet paper on fire in the boys' bathroom, sneaked onto a bus taking *another* class to an art museum, and thereby earned himself a three-day suspension. In this medical analogy, Mrs. Schlom would be a surgeon with a great big sharp scalpel, and an attitude.

Here are the answers to some commonly asked questions about cancer.

Let's say you have cancer and are really depressed and want to drown your trouble in alcohol. What is the worst cancer to have?

That would be Hodgkin's disease, a cancer of the lymph system. People with Hodgkin's disease sometimes get a searing pain in their lymph nodes every time they drink alcohol. No one knows precisely why.

What is the silliest form of cancer?

I would vote for a "chloroma," which shows up as a bright green lump. It can pop up anywhere. A 1970 article in the *New England Journal of Medicine* reported the case of a chloroma patient who had, literally, a green thumb.

Wait a minute. Is that any sillier than a pheochromocytoma?

Maybe not, now that you mention it. Pheochromocytomas usually hit you in the adrenal gland, above the kidney. This causes headaches and heart palpitations and hypertension and, sometimes, strange and overwhelming sensations of anxiety every time you pee.[4]

What is the creepiest form of cancer?

A teratoma. No question. This is a rare tumor that can arise in the male and female gonads. It sometimes has hair or teeth.

What are the two most terrifying words in the whole entire world?

That would be . . . **𝕳𝖊𝖆𝖗𝖙 𝖈𝖆𝖓𝖈𝖊𝖗.**

What? You can get tumors in the heart??!!!???

Yes. And they can be pretty danged wild. The most common tumor that originates in the heart is something called a myxoma, which tends to grow like a blobby round mass from the inside wall of the heart chamber. Sometimes it will plop onto the valve like the float ball in a snorkel, instantly cutting off all blood flow and causing unconsciousness. You are on the precipice of death. Now here's the nifty part: When you collapse, your body goes horizontal. The snorkel ball rolls out of the valve, and you wake up. This is occasionally how myxomas are discovered. They tend to be benign, and can be removed with surgery.

So heart cancer isn't so bad?

Alas, it is. Myxomas are the most common tumors that *originate* in the heart, but they are not the most common tumor of the heart. Most heart tumors are metastases from other body systems, such as the lung, breast, skin, or kidney. By the time they get to your heart, they have spread elsewhere, too. This is very, very discouraging. Medical

---

4. This is actually not the oddest phenomenon involving the act of urination. In "micturition syncope" a miscommunication between the vagus nerve and the blood vessels causes people to faint when they pee. Also, sometimes a tumor or ulcer will open up a hole connecting the colon and the bladder. This will cause people to urinate feces, and sometimes exhibit pneumaturia: farting through the penis.

texts are usually short on adjectives, particularly scary ones: When the news is bad, they typically express this through dry statistics, mortality projections, and nearly incomprehensible prescriptions for last-ditch management ("hemodynamically significant effusions warrant pericardiocentesis to obviate life-threatening cardiac tamponade . . ."). With metastatic tumors of the heart, the textbooks make an exception. The most hopeful-sounding prognosis I found in any book was . . . "dismal."

CHAPTER FOURTEEN

Ulcers and
Other
Visceral Fears

---

*W*hen I turn on my computer, after a series of clicks and groans, a message flashes and asks me if I am aware that my printer is not connected. (I disconnect my printer because it is also a fax machine, and if I keep it always operational, everyone who tries to call me would hear a high-pitched whine, as though this were the answering machine at the residence of Isidore the Bat.) Then another icon comes on to inform me that my sound has been disabled. (I disable my sound because I cannot stomach the "ta-daah!" drumroll that accompanies routine operations, such as reaching the end of a document, because it makes me feel like a four-year-old being extravagantly praised for remembering to flush.) Then my computer tells me it is performing a virus scan, though it has never, to my knowledge, actually found a virus, so this message is pretty much like the *120* on the speedometer dial of a Ford Escort. Then, finally, I try to actually type something and the computer says: ERROR IN WRITING TO FILE—ABORT? RETRY? FAIL?

It is the annoying price we pay for technology. In the world of computers, this is called telemetry. It is the same technology that allowed NASA scientists to have feedback from a spacecraft, complex technical information verified by simultaneous data, so they instantly knew when Alan Shepard, unwilling to postpone a launch, peed in his space suit.

Telemetry is the bane of the hypochondriac. The ordinary person is like an ordinary eighteenth-century piece of farm equipment—say, a wheelbarrow. He operates without much self-awareness. He will know he is in need of repair when his wheel falls off. But the hypochondriac is like a wheelbarrow designed by Microsoft. He has constant two-way communication between his body and himself. He is trying to perform ordinary tasks, such as lumbering up a hill with a load of fertilizer, when suddenly an icon flashes to tell him that rust has been detected on the starboard cotter pin.

One intriguing medical hypothesis is that the hypochondriac is not so much a neurotic as a person who is unusually sensitive to, and in tune with, the mechanics and rhythms of his body. He can actually feel his food digesting and his kidneys manufacturing urine. He is bedeviled by sensations of which other people are unaware.

Nowhere in the body are the incoming signals so prevalent, and so prone to misinterpretation, as in the abdomen. This is because unlike other body systems, the abdomen is a confusing mass of slop, thrown together willy-nilly into a space way too cramped to contain it all. It is like a house that has been flattened by a meteorite. You are likely to find the toilet in the living room. That is what your abdomen is like: Things that have nothing to do with one another are bosom buddies. Your liver is right there next to your lungs. Your spleen is tucked away near a kidney, just down the pike from your descending colon. Food is constantly hurtling around in lumps resembling tumors. Insignificant gurglings are sometimes indistinguishable from life-threatening burblings. It's confusing. The skill and science of diagnosing abdominal problems often involves the very basic matter of fighting off extraneous information to figure out the precise source of your discomfort.

When you went whining to your mother complaining of pain, she asked, "Where does it hurt?" This diagnostic technique operated on the reasonable assumption that if your foot hurt, you probably had something wrong with your foot. Not so with the torso. If the top of your left shoulder hurts, right where an epaulet would be, that could mean you have a ruptured spleen, which is down near the intestines. Really. This is a phenomenon known as "referred pain." To the normal person this medical misdirection is fascinating, but to the hypochondriac it is unnerving. The hypochondriac desperately needs some basic sense of order, some way of limiting his fears to a manageable number of potentially disastrous explanations. If the hypochondriac feels a searing pain in the pit of his stomach, he wants to be fairly sure it is an ulcer, or pancreatic cancer, something vaguely predictable about which he can haunt himself. He does not want an entire vista of other possibilities to open up. He does not want to think that the pain in his stomach might be the first sign of a coronary. But it might be. Heart attacks, particularly serious ones in the lower reaches of the heart, sometimes feel exactly like a perforated ulcer.

Meanwhile, a perforated ulcer can feel exactly like a shoulder strain!

A rupture of the esophagus can feel like a heart attack!

A shooting pain in the back, directly beneath the right shoulder blade, can mean cholecystitis, which is a serious inflammation of the gallbladder. Pain in the lower back and side, radiating to the genitals, can mean kidney stones. Pain when you take a deep breath may have nothing to do with your lungs—you could have peritonitis, a serious inflammation of the membrane that covers the wall of the abdomen; you could also have an infection in the membrane around the liver.

And so it is that when he asks where it hurts, the skilled gastroenterologist sometimes views your answer the way a classy French chef views a kosher dill pickle: mildly amusing, certainly interesting on its own terms, but too gauche to actually, you know, *use*. Books on diagnosis are filled with helpful hints for how to listen to a patient's complaint and then surreptitiously figure out what *really* ails him.

For example, *The Mosby Guide to Physical Examination,* a

bible for the diagnostician, urges the doctor to scrutinize the eyes of the patient as he examines him. If the patient keeps his eyes open, it suggests there may be something seriously wrong. If he keeps his eyes closed, it suggests there isn't.[1] The book also proposes that the doctor offer the patient something tasty to eat; if he is really sick, he probably won't accept. And last, there is the so-called Apley rule: The doctor asks a patient who seems otherwise healthy to point to where it hurts. If he points directly at the navel, the doctor should suspect that the pain is psychosomatic. The farther from the navel the perceived pain is, says the Apley rule, the more likely it is to be organic in origin.

Sometimes localizing your pain is not easy, and a doctor will try to elicit the Markle sign. This is an ancient, primitive test that reeks of quackery. It is one of those things that seem stupid but often work.[2]

Stand straight and rise up onto the balls of your feet, then suddenly relax so your heels hit the floor and jar the body. This can induce pain in the primary area of your problem; it can help diagnose appendicitis, gallbladder disease, diverticulitis, pelvic inflammatory disease in women, and peritonitis.

The gastroenterologist has spent his professional life refining techniques of physical diagnosis; he is skilled in squeezing you and thumping your body and listening for signs of inflammation,

---

1. This is exactly like kissing. If you keep your eyes open when kissing, it means there is something wrong with you. I learned that as a teenager, when I violated the rule and got nailed by my date. She chewed me out. Kissing with one's eyes open, she informed me, was an unmistakable sign of sexual predation; I was a rapist in training. Years passed before I realized that one can be caught at this transgression only by someone who is also kissing with her eyes open. By then my date had become a lawyer. I let it slide.

2. Another is the "pump fake" in football.

or rupture, or fluid buildup.[3] On the one hand, it would be irresponsible and simplistic to attempt to summarize the art and science of abdominal diagnosis in a measly page or two. On the other hand, many popular, critically acclaimed books, such as the Old Testament, also oversimplify. We are told Adam and Eve begat Cain and Abel, and then we immediately learn Cain begat Enoch. Surely they left something out. Was there someone named Betty they didn't tell us about?

If God can oversimplify, who am I to draw a line? '

As he is examining you, your doctor is drawing lines. He is mentally partitioning your body into sections, the way butchers look at a cow and see those dotted lines separating the tenderloin from the rump. Your doctor is imagining a line running vertically from your sternum through your navel to the pubic bone, and a second line horizontally through the navel. This creates four quadrants. To these he adds at least one more region, tracing a circle just below the breastbone, about the dimensions of the top of a coffee can. He has highfalutin clinical names for these regions and their subregions, but the names are arbitrary. We can be arbitrary, too. We will name them after things that can hurt: Love, Hubris, Impulsiveness, Bad Clams, and Kissing a Wall Socket.

Pain in "Love" (Upper-Left Quadrant, Near the Heart)

1. *Ruptured or inflamed spleen.* Look for pallor and intense pain that worsens when the foot of the bed is elevated. Also, pain at the top of the left shoulder. The spleen usually ruptures because of physical injury, but it can become inflamed and painful for many scary reasons.

---

3. Not that he is infallible. Used to be, if you had a stomach ulcer, doctors disdainfully concluded you were the "ulcer type," the sort of feeb who alphabetizes his bookcase and wears tie tacks and makes his bed with hospital corners. You were gently steered toward psychotherapy, and maybe encouraged to find a less stressful job. Now it turns out that more than half of all stomach ulcers are caused by a microbe, *H. pylori.* Your ulcer is probably no more your fault than is an earache, and just as curable. You feel pretty good about this, sort of exonerated, except you have left your job as an investment banker for a career in large-appliance repair.

Tumors can cause an interruption of blood flow to the spleen, causing the death of tissue. A swollen spleen can be a symptom of dozens of treacherous diseases, including leukemia, lupus erythematosus, Hodgkin's disease, polycythemia rubra vera, which attacks the bone marrow, and amyloidosis, a mysterious illness that leads to tremors, fainting spells, heart failure, and death.

2. *Aortic aneurysm,* a ballooning of the wall of the thoracic branch of the body's largest blood vessel. Look for accompanying lower back pain; if this aneurysm ruptures, the pain will become explosive. You are rushed to surgery. It is usually too late. Most victims die from internal hemorrhage.

Pain in "Hubris" (Upper-Right Quadrant)

1. *Liver disease.* Could be cancer or hepatitis, or sometimes both. With hepatitis, look for fatigue, jaundice, lack of appetite, and what medical books cheerfully call "cola-colored urine." By the time liver cancer is diagnosed, it has often spread to or from other body systems, and in that case you are a goner.

2. *Cholecystitis,* an inflammation of the gallbladder. Can be caused by gallstones or infectious disease. Look for relentless pain, vomiting, fever, aching near the shoulder blade.

3. *Leaking duodenal ulcer.* Look for episodic gnawing pain, heartburn, belching.

Pain in "Impulsiveness" (Circle Below the Breastbone)

1. *Perforated stomach ulcer.* Suspect it where there is a history of long-term stomach pain characterized by a dull, burning ache two to three hours after eating. Suddenly this will yield to excruciating pain, cold sweats, gray pallor, vomiting. Untreated, it can lead to peritonitis and death.

2. *Acute pancreatitis.* Look for knifelike pain that seems to bore straight through to the back, and sometimes radiate to the top of the left shoulder. The central pain will later migrate south and toward the right. Sitting and leaning forward lessens the pain. Sometimes the navel dimples inward.

3. *Pancreatic cancer.* Look for weight loss, depression, jaundice, pain in the lower back. Pancreatic cancer has a very, very bad prognosis by the time pain has developed; it often spreads to other systems before it is diagnosed.

4. *Stomach cancer.* Look for a steady ache, radiating to the back.

5. *Volvulus,* a twisting of the intestine on itself, like a Boy Scout's half hitch. Look for pain at the lower reaches of this region, with abdominal distension, nausea, vomiting. This can also kill you if not caught in time.

Pain in "Bad Clams" (Lower-Left Quadrant)

1. *Diverticulitis,* an infection and inflammation of pouches in the large intestine. Look for flatulence and stomach rumbling.

2. *Colon cancer.* Look for severe constipation preceding the pain.

Pain in "Kissing a Wall Socket" (Lower-Right Quadrant)

1. *Appendicitis.* Aching pain, nausea, vomiting, extreme tenderness when one finger is pressed down on the so-called McBurney's point, which is about six inches directly to the right of the navel. Over the previous few days, the pain will have migrated down and to the right, from a few inches below the breastbone.

2. *Regional ileitis (Crohn's disease).* Look for severe pain following diarrhea. This is a debilitating condition of un-

known origin that often requires surgical repair of the intestine, and sometimes a colostomy.

Here are answers to some commonly asked questions about the abdomen.

Can you die of stomach pain?

Yes. Anton Cermak, the mayor of Chicago, was shot to death in Miami in 1933. His assassin, Giuseppe Zangara, told police he had been crazed from the pain of an upset stomach. So, in a sense, Mayor Cermak died of stomach pain. Just not his *own* stomach pain.

I just had a large, greasy meal at Earl's House of Undercooked Poultry. I have a terrible stomachache and nausea. Might I have ptomaine poisoning?

No. There is no such thing as "ptomaine poisoning." Ptomaines are nitrogen compounds that are released by rotting meat, and they were once thought to be poisonous. They are not; in fact, ordinary digestion produces ptomaines in the body. There is probably rotting meat in your intestines right now. I don't know how people can go about their lives knowing that inside their intestines are things that could make a vulture puke. Or what about food in the mouth? How's *this* for a foolproof diet: Every ten seconds during a meal, you are compelled to open your mouth, look in a mirror, and observe the contents before you swallow. How come no one has ever proposed *that* diet?

What is the scariest thing that abdominal pain can mean?

I am not sure I should reveal that. Hypochondriacs might get alarmed.

Oh, c'mon.

OK. Sometimes a person—usually a man in his thirties, forties, or fifties—will feel a dull ache in the "Hubris." He will ignore it. It isn't very severe, and he is a tough guy. Soon he will find that he has a rather nice suntan, even if he isn't out in the sun much. Still, no cause for alarm; this may actually please him. If he is a black person, his skin may lighten, turning a handsome brown-gray, like Ossie Davis. Months or even years may go by. Then the man notices pain in the joints. He starts getting lethargic. Maybe his thinking gets a little confused. His heartbeat becomes irregular. He goes to a specialist. Maybe a cardiologist, for the heart symptoms. Or a rheumatologist, for the joints. Or a gastroenterologist, for the abdominal pain. Or a neurologist, for the mental confusion. Or a dermatologist, for the skin changes. Each specialist suspects and tests for some disease with which he is familiar. Nothing checks out. Months pass. Medical books liken this process to the blind men and the elephant: Everyone sees what he expects to see. No one sees the big picture.

Finally some doctor orders the right test and discovers the patient's blood has more iron in it than the *Lusitania*. The diagnosis will be hemochromatosis, a poisoning of the body by iron overload. It is inherited, but it can be in your family and you might not know it.

Untreated, hemochromatosis can affect virtually every organ in the body. Your knees freeze up with arthritis. Your hips can get deformed, so you walk like a penguin. You get so tired you fall asleep anywhere, in the middle of anything. Your testicles atrophy and you become impotent. Your body softens and loses hair, and you start to look like a woman.[4] Your heart palpitates wildly. You get easily out of breath. Your skin erupts in terrifying spidery bruises. You eventually die of liver cancer, or of painful, suppurating peritonitis, or you bleed to death from ruptured esophageal ulcers.

That's horrible!

No, *this* is horrible: Hemochromatosis is completely treatable if it is caught early enough. Every week or so you get some of your blood

---

4. As distinguished from an arrhenoblastoma, which is a rare ovarian tumor that turns a woman into a man. She gets a deep voice, thick facial hair, flattened breasts, and a rather unnervingly large clitoris.

drained away, and it eliminates the problem. But it is sometimes not caught early enough. Too many doctors wasting too much time.

Fortunately, in the 1980s general practitioners started wising up and catching hemochromatosis because they began ordering iron tests as part of routine blood workups. Unfortunately, in the 1990s some HMOs and other superstingy medical insurers have stopped paying for this test.

In short, look for a spike in the number of cases of runaway hemochromatosis. It will be a sharp spike. It will be made of iron.

CHAPTER FIFTEEN

Are You Too Fat?
Yes. (I Mean,
Look *at* You.)

U sually, medical science is guilty of overcomplicating the simple. But sometimes it oversimplifies the complicated. A case in point is weight control. Medical books and popular health magazines inform us that if you are overweight, it is better to be an pear than an apple—that people who are large of chest and belly have greater incidence of heart disease and diabetes than people built like teardrops.

To find out whether you are apple shaped or pear shaped, take the circumference of your waist one inch above the navel and divide it by the circumference of your hips at the widest point. A normal reading is from 0.7 to 0.85. A higher figure indicates apple obesity; a lower figure indicates pear obesity.

The apple–pear distinction may be true, but it is woefully incomplete, and discriminatory against the differently bodied. What if you are neither an apple nor a pear? Here is an updated list that recognizes and celebrates diversity.

Good	Bad

Tiger

Bear

Yield Sign

Stop Sign

Rectal Thermometer

Poultry Thermometer

Good	Bad

Cheesecake   Urinal Deodorant Cake

But by and large, proper body morphology remains a function of weight.

A few months ago, the medical establishment released a new Optimal Weight Chart, replacing the old system of height and weight with a more complex computation of body mass. This chart appears to have been drawn up by pissed-off feminists. Under these new criteria, perfectly healthy, normal men with slightly stocky bodies—say, your average major-league catcher—are computed to be overweight. Meanwhile, short women get a break. Madeleine Albright is not defined as fat even though she is built—and I do not mean this unkindly—exactly like a scoop of mashed potatoes.

I preferred the old-fashioned weight chart, and urge readers to stick with it:

MEN

Height	Ideal Weight		
	Small-Boned	Medium-Boned	Large-Boned
5'7"	125–190	135–220	140–250
5'8"	130–200	140–240	150–270
5'9"	135–220	145–260	160–290
over 5'9"	140–230	150–280	170–390

WOMEN		
Height	**Ideal Weight**	
	SMALL-BONED	MEDIUM-BONED	LARGE-BONED
5'2"	95	96	97
5'3"	97	98	99
5'4"	99	100	101
over 5'4"	100	102	104

To determine your bone structure, empty a twenty-four-ounce jar of Hellmann's mayonnaise and attempt to place your left hand inside. If it fits easily, you are small-boned. If it does not fit, you are large-boned. If it fits but you cannot remove your hand, you are medium-boned. To remove jar, strike crisply on the edge of a sturdy piece of furniture. If necessary, treat cuts and abrasions with a mild antiseptic to avoid clostridial myonecrosis, also known as "gas gangrene." This is a sudden, sullen, raging infection that attacks open wounds. It causes intense pain, fever, and swelling. The skin turns white and stinks. It oozes brown liquid. If it is untreated, stupor and delirium follow, rapidly progressing to coma.

The coroner will note you were "medium-boned."

CHAPTER SIXTEEN

Snap, Crackle,
and Plop (Minor Aches
and Pains That
Can Kill You)

The other day I was speaking to a colleague of mine, a talented and vastly accomplished professional who, in less enlightened times, might have been described as having excellent hooters. She is one of those women who make it necessary for decent men in the workplace to learn an unnatural method of communication, in which one focuses the entirety of one's apparent attention on the eyes and chin, as though the person to whom you are speaking were a severed head attached to life-sustaining devices.[1]

Like all old, plug-ugly guys, I was using what few meager tools I had to hold her attention—my wisdom, my urbanity, my ability to send this woman on an assignment to Paris if I chose. Things

---

1. This method of communication was first developed by men in the 1970s, when women began breast-feeding as a political act, florping out their personal apparatuses in the middle of restaurants, management training seminars, etc. Fortunately, this practice is on the decline. Now, when women wish to make male coworkers uncomfortable, they weep: copious, rolling torrents of lachrymation, loosed at ludicrously inopportune moments, such as during performance evaluations. Unlike the Breast Florp, the Sudden Weep is not easily countered by a man. There are several strategies, none of them foolproof. You have to do something dramatic to recapture the moment. Some men will wildly applaud. I start speaking in German.

were going swell. Then I made a monstrous error in judgment. To emphasize a point, I stood up.

At the last minute I sensed what was about to happen, but it was too late to stop.

As my behind lifted from the seat, my knee bones began popping like Rice Krispies in seltzer, like bubble wrap being stomped by an epileptic giraffe. I was halfway to my feet, committed. Suddenly aware that I needed to support my ascent with my forearm or risked collapsing back into my seat, I pushed down on the armrest of my chair, causing my elbow to lock, as it sometimes does. This required me to slowly rotate it outward, as though I were performing the disco duck at the bottom of a swimming pool. In so doing, I accidentally knocked off the bookcase and onto the floor a paperweight that is a realistic rubber replica of a prostate gland.[2] Smiling gamely, I bent to retrieve it. Because I am no longer supple enough to bend from the waist, I assumed the junior high school squat-thrust position. Thus situated, I found myself at my colleague's feet, looking up. I said something I hoped was erudite. It might as well have been "ribbit." We would never have Paris.

Medical science has a term for the popping and snapping of aging bone and cartilage. It is called "crepitus." ("Crepitus" also happens to be the official medical term for expulsion of gas from the anus. Medical science can be cruel to the elderly.)

Orthopedics offers mostly discouraging news for the aging, but it is the one area of medicine where I did not expect to have bad news for hypochondriacs. Hypochondriacs thrive on ambiguity. In orthopedics, the problems tend to be straightforward. My friend Steve, for example, is an orthopedic surgeon whose practice is in Colorado, not far from the ski slopes. There is not a huge amount of subtlety in his line of work: People walk in with bones sticking straight out of their stomachs. Even non-ski-

---

2. Don't ask.

related injuries tend to be easily diagnosed. Recently, a guy arrived at Steve's office with an arm problem. The arm arrived separately, in a garbage bag.

Orthopedists anticipate simple, obvious explanations, but sometimes even they are surprised. A pain in the shoulder or above the knee usually is nothing terribly serious. But every once in a while it turns out to be an osteosarcoma, which is a virulent tumor of the bone.

One of the more common complaints an orthopedist fields is lower back pain, and usually this is caused by a muscle strain or a damaged disk in the lumbar portion of the spine. This would be relatively good news. Other causes of lower back pain are tumors of the pancreas or kidney. Those would be worse news. But the worst thing, and it happens from time to time, is metastatic cancer: a malignancy that has spread from another organ, usually the lung or prostate gland or breast. Sometimes you don't know you have these other tumors until they ride the blood to the bone in your spine. The bone grows amok. It starts strangling the spinal cord. By the time you experience the first twinge in your back, it is often too late.

Occasionally, orthopedists will deal with a persistent pain in the lower back or pelvis that is not a simple strain, and not a disk problem, and not a fracture, and not a tumor. It turns out to be the first sign of Paget's disease, an infection that causes abnormal bone growth. It can be particularly evident in the head and face. Your hat size increases. Your features coarsen. You scare young children. You limp. Your bones snap like those oily wonton-soup crackers that, to my knowledge, have no official name.[3] Paget's disease squeezes important nerves. It can make you deaf. It can make you dizzy. It can sometimes make you dead.

Mostly, though, orthopedic surgeons do not make complicated diagnoses. They take pride in the homely tools of their craft. They work with drills and saws and screwdrivers. They are humble carpenters who happen to own vacation chalets in Zurich.

---

3. How about "General Tso's osteosarcoma"?

Diagnosis of musculoskeletal problems often falls to the noble, harried general practitioner, the only doctor who typically gets to know his patient over months and years.[4] This familiarity is important in diagnosing problems like arthritis or rheumatism because these conditions often develop slowly, over time, and people tend to accommodate them by slightly altering their habits. It is like having the brakes in your car slowly fail. You compensate. You start braking a little early. Then you learn to tromp down with both feet. Pretty soon you are veering into shrubbery to slow yourself, and still nothing seems awry. Eventually, you lend your car to your cousin Margaret and she drives off an escarpment.

It is that way with musculoskeletal problems. They tend to sneak up on you.

And so doctors look for subtle behavioral signs of deterioration. They listen for grunts and moans the patient may inadvertently make when performing routine physical activities. Textbooks on physical diagnosis devote pages to recognizing the warning signals in patients who are getting older and may be contracting arthritis or other connective-tissue disease. The list below is adapted from several medical-text sources. It is a scary list, not because it contains terrifying signs but because it doesn't. Everything seems so . . . ordinary.

Action	Normal Activity	Danger Sign	Weakness Indicated
Getting up from dinner table	Push away while seated, sliding chair	Standing first, then pushing chair back with legs or torso	Upper arms
Putting on shirt or cardigan	Reaching behind your back	Putting sleeve on bad arm first, then swinging other sleeve to good arm	Shoulder rotation

---

4. Among doctors, there is a distinct hierarchy in medical specialties. If medical specialties were animals, orthopedic surgeons would be ocelots or jaguars—sleek, elegant animals that might be the pets of international drug dealers. Gastroenterologists would be plow horses, wearing doofy straw hats. Pediatricians are big, friendly, drooly dogs. General practitioners are chiggers.

Action	Normal Activity	Danger Sign	Weakness Indicated
Putting on trousers	Standing	Sitting	Shoulder, upper arm
Picking up item from floor	Bending at waist, squatting	Leaning on furniture for support; use of one hand on thigh to assist raising or lowering torso; resting knee on floor	Knees, pelvis, lower back
Tying shoes	Sitting, resting foot on floor	Use of footstool to decrease spinal flexion	Lower spine
Rising from lying to sitting	Bending at waist, rising straight up	Rolling to one side and pushing with arms to raise to elbows; using furniture to rise to sitting position	Abdominal muscles, lower back
Combing or brushing hair	Head faces forward; brush or comb is maneuvered.	Head is turned to accommodate brush or comb.	Shoulder rotation
Rising from chair	Vertical motion	Upper torso thrusts forward before body rises. Feet spread wide to provide broad base of support.	Lower back, pelvis, knees

After finishing this list, I spent several hours putting on sweaters, getting up from tables, tying and retying my shoes, taking off my pants, forgetting to put them on and alarming the Federal Express man, etc.

Once you know what to look for, if you are inclined toward worry, every motion you make becomes suspect. There are relatively few reliable tests that can help the diagnostician.

> If your doctor suspects hip fracture or dislocation, he may ask you to take your underpants off and stand on one leg. Assuming he is not just having fun at your expense, he is checking for Trendelenburg's sign: With a healthy pelvis, the buttock above the raised leg should be held higher than the other buttock. Persons with breaks or pelvic bone disease cannot do this.

But mostly, diagnosis of musculoskeletal problems is hit-and-miss. Blood tests are not definitive, even for arthritis or lupus erythematosus. It is precisely this subtle nature of musculoskeletal disorders that makes them particularly tempting for the hypochondriac. Diagnosis depends on a highly subjective accounting of what hurts. In short, this is the area in which hypochondriacs can be at their most creative.

Every era contains some musculoskeletal ailment that is characterized by diffuse pain, fatigue, and irritability in the absence of any clear diagnostic evidence of disease. Medical science has always given important-sounding names to these conditions. In the 1800s, patients were diagnosed with "neurasthenia." In the early 1900s, this was upgraded to "neuromyasthenia." In the 1930s there was "myalgic encephalomyelitis." Now all of these illnesses are recognized as quaint artifacts from an unsophisticated past. What silly, gullible bozos we were! Now people get "fibromyalgia."

Fibromyalgia is a trendy disease. It is growing exponentially. Fifteen years ago, it did not exist. In 1990, there were nine hundred thousand reported cases. In 1995, there were 2 million. In many ways, fibromyalgia, like AIDS, is a modern-day pandemic. Perhaps it would be instructive to compare the two ailments.

AIDS. Strikes young, vigorous people in the prime of their lives, sapping them of energy, making them helpless in the face of opportunistic infections, leading to painful skin lesions, malignant sarcomas, neurological impairment, dementia, and death.

Fibromyalgia. Makes you feel icky-doody.

The fibromyalgia sufferer reports tender, achy muscles and joints. He says he has trouble sleeping. His muscles feel stiff. He is tired. He is irascible. He is depressed. He is nervous. He tends to have other vague anxiety-driven disorders, like "irritable bowel syndrome" and "chronic fatigue syndrome." Fibromyalgia doesn't get worse; it just hangs around, like a dingleberry. Also, for some blamed reason it doesn't show up on any chemical tests.

Now, if this sounds like the sufferer of fibromyalgia is a big ol' sissy, that just shows how insensitive you are. If fibromyalgia weren't a real disorder, would doctors be accepting millions of dollars in fees to treat it?

Recently I attended a meeting in Rockville, Maryland, of a support group for persons with fibromyalgia and chronic fatigue syndrome. Rather, I *attempted* to attend the meeting. There were about a dozen people sitting around in chairs, looking tragic. When I said I was writing a book, I was escorted out by a man named Aaron who looked as though he might be a funeral director or possibly a professional airline-crash grief counselor. He informed me that the group was very sensitive about negative publicity; they were afraid they would be portrayed as lazy, whining lunatics. Shocked and insulted, I solemnly assured him that I was a scientist engaged in an objective pursuit of the truth, but he didn't fall for it.

Reputable medical texts tread very, very gingerly around fibromyalgia. Some discount it altogether. Some take it seriously but note delicately that the recommended treatment includes "reassurance" and "frank discussion" and "sympathetic support." The books do give criteria for diagnosing fibromyalgia, identifying eighteen pressure points on the body that show tenderness when pressed with a finger. Supposedly, you cannot diagnose fibromyalgia unless the patient reports pain in eleven of the eighteen points.

Interestingly, not many medical texts give a diagram of these supposed pressure points, and when they describe them they do so in highly technical language ("the left and right lateral epicondyle, the supraspinatus above the scapular line . . ."). I suspect this is deliberate. Doctors know where these points are. If the hypochondriacal patient knew also, he would feel pain wherever he was supposed to.

This leads me to an interesting ethical dilemma. I know precisely where the eighteen diagnostic pressure points are. This book is supposed to be a handbook for hypochondriacs; they are my audience. They have paid for this book. I owe them something. Yet, shall I give them information that might exacerbate their affliction? Dare I tell them where they are supposed to feel pain?

After careful consideration, begun in the previous paragraph, I have reached a decision.

 Here are the pressure points, explained in simple terms:

One immediately inside the point of each shoulder blade, about an inch to the left and right of the spine

Two at the precise points where the schoolyard bully used to pinch you at the top of the back of your neck

One at the very top and center of each shoulder

One beside each elbow on the outside of the body as the arm hangs at your side

One at the outside top of each buttock

One at the center of the abdomen, approximately two inches directly above the navel

One to the side of each knee on the inside portion of the leg

Two at the base of the neck just below and to the left and right of the larynx

Two immediately below and to the left and right of the indentation at the top of the sternum

One beneath the chin, directly under the center of the tongue

There. Now you have it.

Except, there are two pressure points I have not given you. And I made up two that do not exist. If you feel pain there, it will instantly alert any doctor that you are a loon.

Good luck.

CHAPTER SEVENTEEN

Why You
Should Not
Smoke

Medical studies have proven statistically that smoking is linked to lung cancer, oral cancer, bladder cancer, osteoporosis, myocardial infarction, pancreatic cancer, strokes, bronchitis, esophageal cancer, high blood pressure, and for all we know, those chin moles with a single, revolting hair. And yet many hypochondriacs—more aware than most people about medical risks—continue to smoke. Why?

Possibly *because* the evidence is statistical. Ever since Ross Perot took to the airwaves with flip charts the size of queen-size mattresses, mathematically proving that NAFTA would turn us into a nation of earthworm ranchers, prostitutes, and freelance garbagemen, we have learned to mistrust statistics. We know they can be manipulated. We want facts, not figures.

Scientists haven't learned this lesson yet. They scorn so-called anecdotal evidence—individual case studies that may prove their point—because anecdotal evidence is considered unscientific, prone to being emotionalized. So they continue to publish studies that read like this—"The incidence of malignant pulmonary neoplasms, endobronchial lesions and bronchopulmonary sequestrations showed a median increase of forty-six percent in patients who have exhibited sustained alveolar exposure to products containing nicotinated byproducts"—as opposed to this un-scientific, purely anecdotal report published on May 22, 1997, and reprinted here as a public service:

GAINESVILLE, Fla. (AP)—A throat cancer patient died after setting himself on fire trying to light a cigar. He was unable to yell for help because his illness had cost him his vocal cords.

"I don't ever want to witness anything like I witnessed this morning," said Katie Brown, sister of Abraham Mosley. "That will stay with me the rest of my life. He was a walking torch when I woke up."

Mosley, 64, was taken to a hospital Tuesday after the fire but died a short time later.

Confined to a hospital bed in his kitchen, he apparently ignited strips of paper on a stove burner trying to light a cigar because his cancer left him unable to manipulate matches or a lighter. The flaming paper ignited gauze bandages that were around his neck. The fire then spread to his pajamas.

The silent seconds until the smoke alarm sounded may have cost Mosley his life, although officials said he did not have long to live because of his cancer, which was smoking-related.

CHAPTER EIGHTEEN

Pregnant?
That's Wonderful!
Don't Read This!

---

*P**regnancy is a mystical,*** highly complicated physiological state in which the female body responds to timeless genetic imperatives by adapting itself to the arduous, totally natural though repulsive task at hand.

To familiarize yourself with the basic processes of pregnancy, it is helpful to study diagrams of the male and female reproductive systems.

Male Reproductive System

Dick

Balls

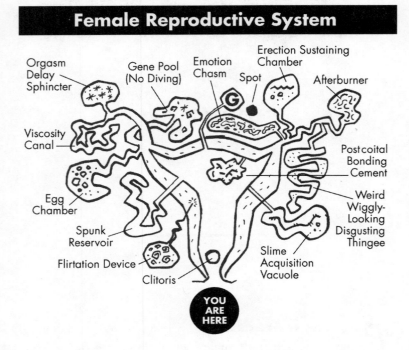

Female Reproductive System

Orgasm Delay Sphincter
Gene Pool (No Diving)
Emotion Chasm
Erection Sustaining Chamber
Spot
Afterburner
Viscosity Canal
Postcoital Bonding Cement
Egg Chamber
Weird Wiggly-Looking Disgusting Thingee
Spunk Reservoir
Slime Acquisition Vacuole
Flirtation Device
Clitoris
YOU ARE HERE

Because women are often mistrustful of male doctors—fearful that men, whatever their book learning, cannot truly understand the process of childbirth—they often do not ask basic questions and remain frightfully ignorant of the totally natural process that is going on. Accordingly, I will now explain pregnancy, for our women readers alone, in a simple, sensitive, accessible, easy-to-understand format.

Basically, there are two stages of pregnancy:

Stage One. You decide to wear that red dress with the back plunge, the one that shows off your behind, and that douche bag Warren keeps hitting on you even after your husband, who ordinarily does not have a jealous, possessive gland in his body, glowers him down a couple of times. Then, at home, you deny anything was going on, while doing that perky Elizabeth Montgomery thing with your nose, and just then, *like it's a total coincidence,* you decide to do leg lifts in your underpants, exposing those crotch-side hollows that don't even have a technical, medical name as far as I know, and then you get pregnant.

Stage Two. You get real fat and your belly button pops out and you give birth to a baby.[1]

The actual birthing process, from a physiological standpoint, consists primarily of grunting and screaming. Insensitive descriptions of the physical difficulty involved, usually by men, include such disagreeable analogies as pulling your lower lip over your nose or fitting a football through a keyhole. This is needlessly alarming. Giving birth is more like pooping a rocking chair.

Fortunately, the birthing process has been made far more civil since the days of the primacy of Natural Childbirth, wherein women were made to feel that if they did not give birth the way Iroquois squaws did in the 1400s, they were somehow less than real women. Nowadays, birth is far more genteel, through the advent of two medical advances: episiotomies and epidural injections.

Episiotomies. At the actual moment of childbirth, to eliminate the possibility of tearing, your obstetrician tears you open with pinking shears. This causes no appreciable pain, in the sense that the chafing of your manacles causes no appreciable pain while the villain is slicing you in half at the sawmill.

Epidural Injections. This is when you get a shot in your back that numbs the lower half of your body. This rather astonishing technomedical innovation lets the woman watch herself give birth almost as a spectator. She knows about the supposed pain of her contractions[2] but does not feel it. This is a great system of giving birth for those women who, through no fault of their own, are candy-asses.

---

1. Unless you give birth to something else. A fabulous 1896 book I found, *Anomalies and Curiosities of Medicine,* reports the case of a woman who experienced a full-term pregnancy and then gave birth to a worm. This book is filled with dubious, poorly documented case histories that should be given little credence, including the case, in Paris in 1830, in which a woman gave birth to a child with three buttocks.

2. Contractions are that physiological process wherein a woman's cervix is dilated preparatory to birth, through hours of excruciating rhythmic pain. When you think about it, this is a highly inefficient system for what is supposedly a completely natural process. It is as though God actually made a mistake.[3] It is as though every time you swallowed food, it caused a searing pain in the eye.

3. Other notable mistakes by God: menstruation, nipples on men, the need to "wipe."

Basically, there are two types of babies:

1. Babies with normal heads. These are delivered by cesarean section.
2. Babies with heads like cucumbers. (Here is an actual picture of my daughter, Molly, moments after her birth.)

Molly is now seventeen. She is a beautiful, brilliant young woman who, as I am writing this, has just walked in the door after a visit to the hairdresser. She appears to have gotten her hair dyed the color of a regulation NBA basketball. I do not know if this is related to her cucumber-head birth; as a scientist, I am just reporting what I see.

For most women, knowledge of one's pregnancy begins with the time-honored ritual of urinating onto one's fingers. Eventually, one hits the strip and it shows a little plus sign. In the ads for home pregnancy tests on TV, this news is usually greeted with a blissful smile and a phone call to one's mother. Beside the phone is a vase of fresh lilacs. Someday I would like to see one of these ads in which the woman looks at the strip, gets up from a mattress on the floor of the basement storeroom she shares with a no-good, tattooed, unemployed shitheel snoring off his crack high beside her, walks to the kitchen, and sticks her head in the oven.

Whether the news is perceived as good or bad, a positive pregnancy test is a sign of health and fertility, unless of course it is a sign you are going to die. This is a fact not usually trumpeted by the makers of pregnancy testing kits. These tests detect the presence of human chorionic gonadotropin, or HCG, which is a hormone that is produced by the placenta. Unfortunately, there is a rare ovarian tumor, called an embryonal carcinoma, that also produces this hormone. So you might not be pregnant at all! You might have a malignancy that can grow to the size of a roll of toilet paper. It is often fatal.

Ordinary, levelheaded women often exhibit subtle signs of hypochondria when they are pregnant, calling their obstetricians at all hours to report mundane bodily events. Such behavior is completely normal, particularly for a first pregnancy. This is because the woman senses that for the first time in her life she is responsible for a life other than her own. The sensitive obstetrician will try to deal with these complaints with patience, gently but firmly reassuring the caller that everything is fine.

Caller: Doctor, I seem to be belching an awful lot.
Doctor: That's perfectly natural.
Caller: Also, I have a sore that won't heal, blood in my stool, sudden weight loss, a mole whose appearance has changed significantly in the last week, and a painless lump under my armpit.
Doctor: That's perfectly natural.

A pregnant woman frequently notices changes in her body that she might find alarming or distressing. These are, however, natural processes, designed to anticipate the wondrous events in her future. The woman and her doctor should work to emphasize their positive aspects. Her breasts will swell and may become sensitive in preparation for lactation, for example; this can be sexually attractive to her husband or partner. Because her appetite increases, and because the fibrous tissues that hold her joints together become slightly more elastic to prepare for childbirth, the pregnant woman's hips might spread so she has the overall muscle tone of a Hacky Sack. Her gross morphology may resemble those plastic punching-bag pop-up clowns with a wad of sand at the bottom. There are men who find this attractive as well; many of them advertise in the back of swingers' magazines, sometimes including Polaroid self-portraits taken in the restroom stalls at bus depots.

Medical books take great pains to emphasize that pregnancy is a totally normal, healthy state. Then they devote entire chapters to explaining how it can complicate virtually every disease the human body is subject to. Pregnancy increases the demands on the pancreas, so a diabetic is vulnerable to dangerous fluctuations in glucose levels. When pregnant, women with kidney diseases like glomerulonephritis can experience kidney failure. Women with sickle cell anemia can get serious infections or congestive heart failure. Women with heart disease have been known to bring a baby to term, give birth, and then die. Pregnancy can dramatically intensify the symptoms of lupus erythematosus, rheumatoid arthritis, and multiple sclerosis. Pregnancy typically elevates blood pressure, so a woman with hypertension will sometimes have a stroke. A fetus can also dangerously complicate diagnosis: Because the fetus pushes the appendix up, when pregnant women get appendicitis, the pain is not where it customarily is. It seems to be gas or normal abdominal cramping; this can lead to a delay in treatment, and sometimes a life-threatening crisis of peritonitis.

Here is a listing of symptoms sometimes exhibited by the pregnant woman. In column 2 are the most likely explanations. In column 3 are the most terrifying explanations. Hypochondriacs are urged to ignore column 3.

Symptom	Most Likely Explanation	Most Terrifying Explanation
Nausea, vomiting	You are pregnant.	You have serious hyperemesis gravidarum, an imbalance of fluids and electrolytes. This may require hospitalization and sometimes abortion. Also, you might have a gastric tumor. Sometimes this can grow to the size of a schnauzer.
Breast lumps	You are pregnant.	You have breast cancer. Lumps caused by the ordinary processes of pregnancy, such as enlargement of the milk ducts, resemble some tumors. Even experienced obstetricians sometimes get confused. The delay in diagnosis can kill you.
Swollen ankles	You are pregnant.	You have preeclampsia, a serious elevation of blood pressure in the third trimester. If untreated, it can lead to eclampsia, which can result in seizures, strokes, abortion, or death.
Fatigue	You are pregnant.	You have thyroid disease, congestive heart failure, hepatitis, or pernicious anemia, which involves a deficiency of vitamin B_{12}. This last one is particularly insidious because it features additional symptoms that mimic symptoms of pregnancy, including constipation and tingling in the limbs. Therefore, it can go undetected in a pregnant woman. Worst-case scenario: degeneration of the spinal cord, madness, and death.

Symptom	Most Likely Explanation	Most Terrifying Explanation
Shortness of breath	You are pregnant.	You have a lymphatic tumor in the mediastinum, which is the area between the lungs. Because your fetus cannot survive chemotherapy, you may have to choose abortion, or if you prefer it because of your moral or religious beliefs, death.
Watery discharge	You are pregnant.	You are not pregnant. You have a tubal carcinoma, which is a cancer of the fallopian tubes.
Spotting; bloody discharge	You are pregnant.	You are pregnant, but you are not carrying a baby. You are carrying a "hydatidiform process," which is a big, hairy mole.

And finally, some commonly asked questions about pregnancy.

Do you think some women milk their pregnancies just a little too much, making their husbands run out in the rain at nine o'clock at night to pick up some nauseating combination of food, like blueberry yogurt and sardines, and then bursting into tears when you suggest, real politely, an alternative snack, God forbid she should have to eat tuna fish?

No.

How did you, personally, discover what female genitalia look like?

I was approximately eleven years old and went to the bathroom in a doctor's office. On the wall, discreetly placed, was a card with an illustrated diagram showing men and women how to use a sterile towelette before giving a urine sample. The illustration was extremely clinical, but also extremely detailed. I stole the card.

Is that the only thing you ever stole? In your life?

I believe so.

What is the funniest headline ever published?

That would be the headline printed in the *Bucks County* (Pa.) *Courier-Times* in 1977, above a medical story: CERVICAL CANCER CAN BE LICKED.

I am a pregnant woman. Can you please scare the hell out of me?

Sure. The birth of grotesquely abnormal fetuses is a rarity, but it is common enough that there are dozens of clinical Latin medical terms for fetal monsters. Most are born dead. Here are the top ten:

Harlequin: Looks like a hippopotamus. Skin is covered with thick, horny scales and plates.

Acephalobrachia: Lacks both arms and a head.

Cephalomelus: Arm or leg protrudes from head.

Cephalothoracopagus: Twins united at the head and neck and chest.

Cryptodidymus: Twins in which one fetus is hidden entirely within the body of the other.

Hemicephalus: Half a brain.

Hemiacephalus: No brain.

Holocardius amorphus: A blob.

Holocardius acephalus: No heart, head, or chest.

Holocardius acormus: Just a head.

CHAPTER NINETEEN

Things That
Can Take
Out an Eye

―――――――

Go to the bathroom and get your toothbrush. Open your right eye. Now, using a vigorous side-to-side motion, brush your eyeball.

You didn't do it, did you? People are squeamish about their eyes, particularly hypochondriacs. Hypochondriacs do not think of the eyeball as just another organ. They think of it as an extremely vulnerable object that, in a disastrous design error, was placed right out in front of the body, as though Toyota accidentally made the bumper of the Corolla out of Limoges. Hypochondriacs think the eye is like a water balloon and that any puncture of it will result in a sickening pop, a gush of viscous fluids, and permanent blindness.

Don't worry. The eyeball is more like a firm green grape. Try an experiment. Get a firm green grape. Now take a pin. Puncture it. See, it does not explode! Now take a razor and slit the grape horizontally, about halfway through. See? Just a little leakage. It sort of looks like Oscar the Grouch![1] In fact, the eye sometimes be-

―――――――――――――――

1. It is a little-known fact that during eye surgery, doctors often take your slit eyeball and flap it open and shut while talking in little squeaky voices, to relieve tension.

haves like one of those self-healing tires, which repair their own punctures.

OK, still with me? Now, take the grape and sit on it.

My point is, don't press your luck. The eye is not indestructible. Though a simple, small puncture won't usually kill it, trauma with a blunt object will.

Remember how your sainted mom always issued dire warnings about things that could take out an eye, such as BBs from Daisy air rifles, darts, rocks, and harpoons? Well, we mean no offense, but your sainted mom was an idiot. These things sometimes took out eyes, but less often than you might think, precisely because everyone *expected* them to take out eyes and approached them with a basic degree of caution. The things that *actually* take out eyes are far more interesting.

Below is a list of actual things that have recently taken out an eye, compiled exclusively for this book by the Helen Keller Eye Research Foundation[2] in Birmingham, Alabama:

1. A chicken beak.
2. A turnip, pulled from the ground in a reckless manner.
3. A supermarket laser scanner. The customer apparently placed his eye on the glass for a look-see.
4. A pine cone falling from a tree on a recumbent person.

To this list, I would have to add hog slop and potato bazookas. I did not know about these things until recently, when I spoke with Dr. Lorenz Zimmerman, a famous eye pathologist in Washington, D.C., who has studied eye injuries and knows a million of them. He mentioned one tragic case in which a farmer got some hog slop in his eye. Hog slop is not produced with the fastidiousness one might associate with the production of, say, a vial of tetracycline. The eye got infected and the farmer went blind. The most lurid case Dr. Zimmerman knew of occurred in upstate

---

2. A reputable organization that cooperated with me because I implied I was researching a serious medical book. Ha ha.

New York a couple of years ago. It was a classic potato bazooka incident.

A potato bazooka is a highly scientific homemade weapon that makes use of the volatility of hair spray and the structural integrity of PVC pipe to launch a potato the length of a football field. Potato bazookas are sometimes used by bucktoothed morons to hunt rabbit or squirrel. In this case, the individual apparently attempted to utilize this instrument in his living room. Alcohol was involved.

To better understand the vast array of things that can go wrong with your vision, it might be instructive to review How the Eye Works.

When we were in grade school, we learned the eye works by bringing an idea to a committee, which schedules public hearings in a timely fashion. Or possibly that is How a Bill Becomes a Law. Now that I think of it, we learned that the eye works like a camera. Recently I discovered that this is basically true. This came as a shock because most of what we were taught in grade school involved preposterous oversimplifications, due to the standard textbook requirement of reducing everything to simple numbered lists that can be memorized. (Reasons for World War II: 1. Hitler, 2. economy, 3. naval superiority, 4. Asia.) So you can imagine my surprise when I learned that, indeed, the eye works like a camera.

The image comes in through the lens, and it is projected back through the vitreous humor[3] onto the retina. You cannot see your retina any more than you can taste your tongue, but you can sort of see what your retina looks like when an ophthalmologist shines a bright light on it and you see a reflection. It is a tangle

---

3. Despite its name, there is nothing funny about the vitreous "humor," except, possibly, the fact that it is odorless. So it is without any scents. No scents. Of humor. Then again, perhaps this is not funny.[4]

4. On the other hand, the humerus, which is the bone extending from the shoulder to the elbow, ends in the "funny bone." Doctors find this hilarious. In general, doctors have unbelievably lame senses of humor. Their concept of cutting-edge comedy is *Reader's Digest*'s "Laughter, the Best Medicine" page, featuring jokes such as: "Patient: I have a pain in my upper-arm bone. Doctor: That's 'humerus.' Patient: You wouldn't think so if it was you."

of capillaries against a sea of angry pink flesh. It is interesting that whatever you are looking at—a vista of breathtaking natural beauty, the face of a loved one beckoning to you in soft seduction—is processed through this screen that looks like highway raccoon viscera. Plus, the image is reflected upside down:

The Eye

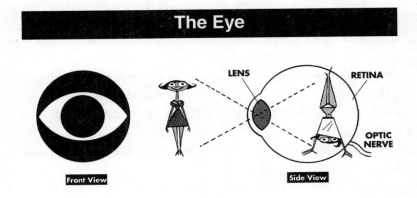

Front View   Side View

The two most common eye problems are nearsightedness and farsightedness, which are caused by minor defects in the shape of the eyeball. The normal eyeball is 23.5 millimeters long. The nearsighted one is longer; the farsighted one is shorter. How can you tell if you are nearsighted or farsighted? One way would be to pop out your eyeball with a soup spoon and measure it. A better method would be to go to a mirror and look at your face, specifically that portion of your face visible behind your glasses. If it looks as though your head has been immersed in pickle brine for several years until it got as small as an egg, then you are nearsighted. If your eyes look huge, like one of those paintings by famed 1960s incompetent Walter Keane, then you are farsighted.

I am nearsighted. Once, for about forty-five minutes, I thought this was a blessing. At the time, I was lying on the floor of a small cabin in Vermont on a cold winter day. Inches before me was a glass of claret, nearly empty, its stem sunk deep into the russet pile of the carpet. The orange flush of a roaring fire was dancing on the belly of the glass. It was beautiful, and it was all I saw clearly. The rest of the room was a warm blur. I felt alone in an elegant old photograph, a tintype with softened borders.

I had removed my eyeglasses and could not see anything to mar the elegance of that scene. I couldn't see the toilet in the distance. I couldn't see the unmade bed. I couldn't see the pizza box with the ruins of dinner. At this moment, my world was a blissful distortion of closeness. Also, I was pitifully drunk.

I contemplated my great good fortune. Only the nearsighted could truly understand the comforting intimacy of their affliction, I thought. Only the nearsighted can remove their glasses and be suddenly, profoundly alone with the book they are reading or the person they are loving. As I lay there on the cabin floor, I felt inspired. I would write a book. It would be an ode to imperfect vision, a work of art, of poetry. A title leapt to mind: *Myopia Utopia.*

The fire died out. I drifted off to sleep, flushed with wine and wisdom.

In the morning I awoke and changed my mind. That is because once I got my glasses on I could see that while I had lain there, enraptured, planning my literary coup, a huge ember from the fire had leapt out and plopped onto the floor not ten feet away. Right before my eyes, it had slowly sizzled a four-inch hole through the carpet and into the floorboards. I had to pay the innkeeper extravagantly for the damage. I did not write the book.

In the last twenty years, medical science has developed a surgical procedure called "radial keratotomy" to cure defects in vision. The procedure is relatively simple, if terrifying: The outer lining of the eye, called the cornea, is cut by knife or laser and reshaped to compensate for a misshapen eyeball. The operation corrects bad vision, particularly myopia.

My friend Karl recently went to a doctor to inquire about radial keratotomy. Karl has been myopic his whole life and is sick of it. He was concerned about the pros and cons of the procedure, possibly because places that do radial keratotomy make you sign elaborate waivers, thick forms that look like what you used to have to fill out to obtain airline flight insurance, where it listed potential damages with unnerving specificity, such as "$200,000 for the loss of one arm, both legs, and one ovary; $205,000 for the loss of one arm, both legs, and *both* ovaries," etc.

Karl wanted reassurance. He wanted to be convinced of the doctor's professionalism. So he sat down with her and inquired about the risks of the procedure.

The doctor told him that the only conceivable danger is that the operation cuts away about 10 percent of the cornea of the eye.

"And . . . ?" Karl asked.

The doctor leaned forward. "Well, have you ever been in a bar?"

"Yes," Karl said.

"Well, imagine that the guy next to you is drunk, and gets nasty, and he takes a beer bottle and smashes it against the bar, and then swings at your face with the broken bottle."

"OK," Karl said.

"Well, imagine that he strikes you in the eye."

"OK," Karl said.

"Well, you will have ten percent less protection against eye injury."

Karl waited. Just silence.

"That's it?" Karl said.

"That's it."

"So," Karl asked, "what is your advice?"

"My advice is to stay out of bars."

Karl got the surgery.[5]

In the last few months, I have been reading extremely complicated medical books, and I must say that as a professional editor, I find them frustrating. These books were written by doctors, not writers, so they have no sense of pacing, character development, or drama. Here is a small example: Several sections on ophthalmological diseases point out that it is possible to contract gonococcal conjunctivitis—basically, gonorrhea of the eye—from contact between your eyeball and your partner's infected genitalia. That's it. That's all the detail they supply! Then they go on to something else! This would be like ending *Casablanca* before Rick tells Louis whose names to put on the letters of transit. The credits would be rolling, Ilse and the weenie Victor Laszlo would

---

5. Karl is not renowned for his superior judgment. He has done other dumb things. He is the only person I know who once slammed a car door on his own head.

be standing around in that phony fog, and everyone in the audience would be saying, "Huh? Wait a minute! Do some people have sex with their eyeballs?"

The single most common complaint about the eye involves "floaters," which I dealt with briefly in Chapter 6. Floaters move sluggishly across your field of vision, halfheartedly trailing the play, like the fat kid in the defensive backfield. They are almost always no cause for concern, unless you suddenly notice an increase in them. A sudden increase in floaters can mean your retina is detaching, or it could be the first sign of retinitis, an early complication of AIDS.

Even though ophthalmology is one of the most sophisticated medical specialties, involving the use of high-tech futuristic equipment one would expect to find on the assembly line at Spacely Sprockets, there are a number of decidedly low-tech physical tests that can be used in basic diagnosis. To the practicing ophthalmologist, these would seem horribly primitive; asking him to perform them would be an insult, like asking the chief justice of the United States Supreme Court to represent you before Judge Judy.

Even though these tests seem to work.

Let's say you have noticed a slight deterioration in your visual acuity. If you go to an ophthalmologist, he will perform various tests on you, some of which require him to dilate your pupils so you look like Little Orphan Annie. A far simpler test exists that can quickly indicate whether your vision problem is simple or potentially more troublesome.

 Take a thin piece of cardboard. Make a pinhole in it. Now look through the pinhole without glasses or corrective lenses. If your vision problem is due to simple refractive error—nearsightedness or farsightedness—your eyesight will improve slightly when you look through the hole: You need glasses, or a change in your current prescription. This is because the pinhole blocks light waves coming in from the sides, which are the light waves that are most subject to distortion by a lens. But if your eyesight does not get any better when you peep through the hole, this is a sign of more serious problems, like neurological impairment or, more likely, the beginning of macular degeneration, which is a slow deterioration of the center of the retina. Eventually, to see anything at all, you will have to try to look away and catch a glimpse of it at the periphery of your vision. This is not easy. A 1977 Chevy Nova, for example, might resemble a water buffalo.

One of the initial signs of problems with your thyroid gland, or a sign of a tumor in the nasal sinuses, is a condition called proptosis, which is a bulging of the eyeballs. This happens so gradually you may not recognize it. After a while you will just seem a little startled all the time, like Loni Anderson after a recent facelift. There is a complex device called an exophthalmometer that doctors use to measure eye bulge, but a far simpler, ancient diagnostic test seems to work quite reliably. It is called Joffroy's sign.

 Tilt your head down, to look at the floor. Now, without moving your head, look up toward the ceiling. Your forehead should wrinkle. If it does not, you may have proptosis.

Have your eyes been hurting? Are they red? The good news would be conjunctivitis, which is a relatively minor infection treatable by pharmaceuticals. Worse news would be glaucoma, an increase in pressure within the eyeball that can ultimately lead to blindness. You might also have a serious condition called anterior uveitis, an inflammation of the iris and surrounding tissues. This also makes your eye hurt. If you suspect it, try this:

 Close the eye that seems to be worse. Shine a flashlight into the open eye. If you feel pain *in the closed eye,* that is a positive sign for anterior uveitis. This is called the Au-Henkind test, and it is said to be nearly 100 percent reliable.

Anterior uveitis has many causes, but it can be an initial sign of awful diseases, including ankylosing spondylitis, which is, literally, a huge pain in the ass. Ankylosing spondylitis attacks in the buttocks, then spreads up the spine. It can create crippling deformities. Anterior uveitis can also signal Behcet's syndrome, which leads to fiery ulcers of the mouth and genitals, and sometimes arthritis, phlebitis, encephalitis, arterial disease, and fatal pulmonary embolisms.

That's the alarming thing about the eyes: Eyes depend on the proper functioning of a delicate lattice of capillaries, and therefore various systemic illnesses that affect the blood can show up there first. Almost every symptom can mean either a minor problem or a major problem. Isn't that exciting, hypochondriacs?

Symptom	Most Likely Diagnosis	Most Terrifying Diagnosis
Red, scratchy eyes	You have conjunctivitis, a minor infection, treatable with antibiotics.	You are showing one of the first symptoms of Reiter's syndrome, a rare and mysterious condition that leads to severe urinary problems and recurrent and sometimes permanent crippling arthritis.
Indistinct sight, particularly in the center of your field of vision	You have floaters.	You have macular degeneration. You will slowly go blind.
Eye discharge	You have conjunctivitis.	You have onchocerciasis, which is river blindness, caused by the bite of black flies that deposit worms in you.[6]
Drooping eyelid, called "ptosis"	You have a minor eyelid infection.	You have myasthenia gravis. It can turn you into flaccid goop.

6. Worms cause all sorts of diseases, and they enjoy the eyes. Loiasis, for example, is an infestation of the loa loa worm. It spreads throughout your body but is often not diagnosed until the worms are seen migrating across your eyeball.

Symptom	Most Likely Diagnosis	Most Terrifying Diagnosis
Lump on eyelid	You have a chalazion, a papilloma, or a xanthelasma, none of which is as serious as it sounds.	You have a basal cell carcinoma or a blepharoatheroma. These are as serious as they sound. If they are caught early enough, you will survive with surgery, but your eyelid may get a little gnarly looking, like genitalia.
Pupils of unequal size	You have benign mydriasis, a harmless condition.	You have tabes dorsalis, usually linked to syphilis. It causes an inexorable deterioration of the spinal column. You start walking stupidly, like a drunken drum major. Then you lose control of your bladder and sexual function.
Double vision, with light sensitivity	You have chorioretinitis, which usually clears up.	You have botulism, which sometimes doesn't.
Double vision	You have a minor imbalance in the strength of the muscles around the eye.	You have an inoperable brain tumor, or a cerebral hemorrhage, or meningitis, or encephalitis, or diphtheria.
Cloudy vision	You have a cataract.	You have interstitial keratitis. It is a sign of many diseases, including leprosy.

Here are some commonly asked questions about the eye:

Why do some women paint their eyelids the color of egg-plants? Do they think this looks good?

This is not strictly a medical question, though the overuse of eye shadow, mascara, and other eye makeup can create corneal ulcers and exacerbate allergic reactions; this is why makeup companies must test their products by rubbing them on rabbit eyeballs until the eyeballs explode. Some men find purple eye shadow attractive. These men tend to have their first names ("Wayne") stitched over their shirt pockets at work.

What happens to the eyes when you get to be middle aged? What is that all about?

Here is an interesting diagnostic test anyone can perform. Go to some public place, like a park or playground. Find someone who is attempting to read a book but holding it at arm's length. This person will be experimenting with different distances and squinting. He will look as though he were attempting to play a slide trombone. Then walk up to this person and say, "I bet you are exactly forty-two years old."[7] Chances are you will be correct. This is because at almost exactly forty-two, the eye loses a certain amount of elasticity. This condition is called "presbyopia." When my friend John Pancake was forty-eight he actually purchased *trifocals*, which leads to the obvious follow-up question:

What kind of a name is John Pancake?

This book may be tasteless, but I draw the line at making fun of someone's name. I "flatly" refuse to do so.

Remember "X-ray Specs," those $2 glasses for sale in the back of 1950s comic books that supposedly let you see through ladies' clothing? Has anyone actually invented such a product?

---

7. Do not do this if the person is clearly not forty-two. Do not do this if the person appears to be, say, eighteen, especially if this person is a woman.

No one has invented such a product, nor will anyone.

Is that because no one would buy a product that would violate people's privacy in such a shameful way?

Don't be ridiculous. It won't be invented because it won't work well enough. I talked to experts in the field of sonar and infrared technology, who agreed it would be possible, and not terribly difficult, to create a visual scanner that could penetrate clothing, survey the contours of the skin below, and transmit it back to a computer, which would use an algorithm to create a realistic, skin-toned image that could be projected on a mini-computer contained within a pair of glasses. Henry E. Bass, distinguished professor of physics at Mississippi State University and director of the National Center for Physical Acoustics, estimates such a product, if it were available commercially, would cost about $1,500. No problem, for the motivated pervert. The problem is a built-in design flaw. "Pubic hair is not that much different from clothing," Dr. Bass says. "If you are able to eliminate one, it would be hard to see the other. That's gonna be tough."

To summarize: Fifteen hundred dollars. No pubic hair.

No X-ray Specs.

What is that pink thing in the corner of the eye? Why, in old people, does it look like worm larva?

It is called the "lachrymal caruncle." It is one of those organs whose function is to go unnoticed for years and years until one day you really look at it, and it totally grosses you out. Another one of these is the uvula. Most people never think about the uvula, dangling in the back of the throat, bobbling back and forth unnoticed, forgotten, until some idiot makes you aware of it. Then some people become obsessed with it. They imagine they can feel it all the time, whapping against the throat, stimulating the gag function, interfering with the swallowing of food, a constant, malignant presence that CANNOT BE IGNORED AND MUST BE ELIMINATED EVEN RIGHT NOW, WITH ANYTHING YOU CAN FIND INCLUDING TOENAIL CLIPPERS OR A STAPLE REMOVER. Fortunately, this rarely occurs.

CHAPTER TWENTY

Oh, Crap
(Diagnosis by the Process of
Elimination)

I **work at** *The Washington Post,* which is a great and powerful
news organization that will boldly publish stories that infuri-
ate potentates, put people in prison, provoke multimillion-dollar
libel suits. But certain subjects scare it half to death. Like every
big, respectable newspaper, it fears being labeled "tabloid."[1] And
so it is that several months ago, *Post* editors killed a story by one
of their finest foreign correspondents because the subject matter
was considered vulgar.

Fulfilling my duty under the First Amendment to eradicate
censorship and suppression wherever it arises, I am now going to
disclose for the first time the contents of this story: Women in
Japan suffer from terrible constipation because they are embarrassed to move their bowels.[2]

This is true. They won't leave their desks at work because people will watch them, calculate the amount of time it took them to
return, and surmise what they have been up to. Constipation

---

1. The editors at big, gray newspapers like *The New York Times* try mightily to
maintain a sense of decorum and stiff formality, even at the risk of sounding hopelessly
fuddy-duddy, such as by referring to Snoop Doggy Dogg as "Mr. Dogg."

2. The story quotes a doctor who specializes in this problem. His name is Dr.
Ikeshita.

during honeymoons is epidemic because women are worried about what they might reveal of themselves to their new spouses in the close quarters of a hotel room. Once married, Japanese women typically will wait for their husbands to leave for work before they use the toilet. A hot-selling item in Japan is a bathroom accessory for women delicately called the Sound Princess, which produces pleasing nature sounds[3] to cover up distressing body noises.

Now, what can we learn from this?

First, stories like this one provide a valuable cultural lesson. Every time we think we have finally figured out that the earth is one great big comfy living room filled with people exactly like us and we should all be nice to everybody because they are our siblings united in the blissful commonality of humanity, we read that in, say, Yemen, jaywalkers are beheaded.[4]

The second lesson is that the human body has astonishing control over its bowels. If you can induce constipation as an act of will, then you can do almost anything. A hypochondriac's playground!

Before proceeding, let me say that it is easy to find adolescent humor in normal bodily processes, and this is a good time to, heh heh, rectify the situation. There is nothing funny about hawking up a loogie or making foof-foof noises from the rump hole.[5] The fact is, bodily secretions are so natural that some of them have even been commemorated in song. One example is eye crud ("Mr. Sandman," by the the Chordettes, 1954). Another is vaginal discharge, and it is a perfect example of how one might go "a little too far" in the pursuit of humor. In his song, Frank Zappa advocated stealing women's panties and wearing them on one's head as "discharge party hats." God was as appalled as you are. Mr. Zappa is dead.

---

3. The sounds of babbling brooks, chirping larks, etc. Wouldn't it be great if every fifteen minutes or so the Sound Princess emitted an EXTREMELY LOUD fart?

4. *The World Almanac* provides a terrific antidote to sugary we-are-the-world fantasies. We are not the world. The world is dorky. In Equatorial Guinea, the two main ethnic groups are the "Fangs" and the "Bubi." The leader of Gabon is "President Bongo." The entire economy of Djibouti is listed as "salt."

5. Am I the only one who has noticed that the British novelist John Mortimer, known for his urbanity, created a detective whose name, basically, is Rump Hole?

I had Zappa's demise in my head the day I went to interview one of Washington's most distinguished colorectal surgeons, Dr. Bruce Orkin. I resolved to approach the topic of pooping with all the restraint and reverence one might associate with an ecumenical council.

Dr. Orkin arrived fresh from surgery, in a white lab coat. It was very clean. I had many things that I wanted to ask Dr. Orkin, things that had been bedeviling me my whole life, such as why toilet paper comes in squares so small no one can use only one.[6] But I did not ask this. I was asking very mature questions, and Dr. Orkin was answering in a very mature fashion, both of us hewing maturely to the notion that there is nothing remotely funny about the colon, or the rectum, or human intestinal function. Dr. Orkin was going on about the need for roughage (it is very, very important) when I suddenly interrupted to ask him about something I could not get out of my mind. I did not know how to broach the subject in an appropriately stately fashion, so I just handed him a copy of a 1987 medical abstract from the *American Journal of Forensic Medicine and Pathology*. This story had made the rounds of the *Post*. It had stains on it, drool marks from where coffee was launched out of people's noses, etc. The article described a case in which a man came into an emergency room complaining of rectal pain. Doctors discovered a huge, hard mass in his rectum. The man initially claimed he did not know how this object got there, but in time he admitted he'd had his boyfriend pour wet concrete into his anus with a funnel, and (surprise!) it hardened, forming a rocklike object that doctors had to remove, like delivering a baby. The object was six inches long, four inches thick, and contained, imbedded at the far end, perfectly intact . . . a Ping-Pong ball.[7]

---

6. I recently learned there is an actual answer to this: Toilet paper squares are small not because anyone is expected to use just one but because some people use two, and some use three, and this is the only way of accommodating both types of clientele. Seriously. Entire scientific studies have been done on this by the toilet paper industry.

7. There is something about this story that propels normal, decent people into uncharacteristic excesses of sophomoric humor. When I showed it to my friend Pat, who is a Sunday school teacher, the mother of two young children, and an authority on the proper use of the English language, she said, and I quote: "Kind of gives new meaning to the term 'shitting a brick.' "

Dr. Orkin scanned this article. "Oh," he said.

He looked at me dourly. I sensed I had made a terrible mistake. I sensed the interview was about to be terminated.

"Let me show you something," Dr. Orkin said.

Abruptly, his demeanor changed. Rising from his desk with new animation, he went to a file cabinet and extracted a set of keys from his pocket. Then he pulled from the wall a large vertical slide cabinet, the type doctors on *ER* use to display X-rays of hearts and lungs and broken bones. It was entirely filled with small slides. There were perhaps seventy-five of them.

On almost every slide was something that Dr. Bruce Orkin, eminent colorectal surgeon, had personally removed from a rectum. Usually, there was a "before" and an "after": objects photographed in situ, through an X-ray, and then again after extraction. There were photos of bottles, vibrators, and lightbulbs. One was of a gigantic, realistic black rubber penis roughly the dimensions of a meatball sub. One showed a delicate French glass vase. (In the "after" picture, a yellow rose had been placed in it. An elegant touch.) "Actually," corrected Dr. Orkin, "that one was removed by my colleague Dr. Sackier."

One photo showed a bottle of Suave roll-on deodorant. That patient had come in with his wife, Dr. Orkin recalled. She grumped that the bottle had been too smooth, offering nothing to hold on to.[8]

One photo showed someone with *two* lightbulbs in his butt.

"Why would you put *two* lightbulbs in you?" I asked.

"If one is good, two is better." Dr. Orkin shrugged.

I am not an expert in anatomy, but one of the pictures appeared to be of a penis, not a rectum. Inside the penis, quite clearly, was a chicken bone[9] broken in two. Dr. Orkin is a rectum man.

"A friend gave me that one," he explained.

"You like this stuff?" Dr. Orkin asked a little unctuously, like a playground dope pusher. I nodded; at this point, I was speechless. Then the doctor produced another key. He opened another

---

8. *Note to deodorant manufacturers:* Consider handgrip.
9. Giving rise, presumably, to the term "boner."

drawer. He extracted from it an object swathed in a towel, and handed it to me. It appeared to be about the size of a railroad spike. It appeared to weigh about as much as a railroad spike. "It has been cleaned," Dr. Orkin assured me.

I unwrapped it.

It was a railroad spike.

It was ten inches long, an inch and a half thick, with a sharp end. "I took it out of the descending colon," Dr. Orkin said.

Dr. Sackier walked by. I complimented him on the vase, and he blushed and stammered, and said that really, it was nothing compared with the fine work Dr. Orkin has done.

"Did he show you the railroad spike?"

Jonathan Sackier is a Brit, and so everything he says sounds dignified and magisterial, which is particularly entertaining when he is discussing his study entitled "Management of Colorectal Foreign Bodies." In this, Dr. Sackier follows up on forty-nine selected cases of foreign objects up the gazoo, including fourteen vibrators, eight dildos, three wooden dowels, three vegetables (type unspecified), three bars of soap, three deodorant bottle tops, two deodorant bottles, one porcelain teacup, one television vacuum tube, one glass bottle, one marble egg, five ballpoint pens (apparently inserted together), one chicken bone (!), one handle of garden shears, one screwdriver, one cigar tube, one Lucozade bottle, and one "packet of white powder." The range of objects inserted, Dr. Sackier notes, "is not limited by the imagination, but by the size of the rectum."[10]

All of this carries a valuable object lesson: Don't try to stick any object in your rump that is smaller than an unabridged thesaurus, or you might wind up on your belly in a room full of giggling people with forceps.

This is not to suggest that intestinal specialists spend all their time extracting items from people's behinds. Every few weeks they apparently take a break to treat someone else, often some-

---

10. This is not a recent development. In a pioneering 1934 thesis, famed British colorectal surgeon J. P. Lockhart-Mummery dryly pointed out that any object that can be inserted in the rectum has, at some time, been removed. Lockhart-Mummery dealt delicately with the subject. Autoeroticism was not mentioned; he accepted the patients' explanations for their predicament, including attempted relief from itching and accidents of a most unfortunate nature ("I was gardening naked when . . .").

one diagnosed with "irritable bowel syndrome." Irritable bowel syndrome is the cash cow of the gastrointestinal industry. Victims report intestinal pain coupled with alternating bouts of diarrhea and constipation. There is no obvious cause. Irritable bowel syndrome is one of those modern diseases that can best be described by what they are not rather than what they are. Other examples are "noncardiac chest pain" and "nonulcer dyspepsia." All three conditions cause vague symptoms that are not clearly linked to organic problems, that seem related to stress and anxiety, and that don't seem to show up in ordinary chemical tests, which implies that either (1) medicine has not yet determined the cause of these conditions or (2) these conditions are horse potatoes. As it happens, there is a dramatic overlap of patients who have irritable bowel syndrome and those with nonulcer dyspepsia or noncardiac chest pain. I personally draw no conclusions from this. I hereby declare irritable bowel syndrome to be a real, live, genuine, terrible scourge, mostly because I do not want to be picketed by angry persons with gas.

Diseases in most bodily systems can cause a wide array of symptoms. This is not true with the intestines. Intestinal disorders tend to show up as either constipation or diarrhea, which greatly simplifies things for the hypochondriac.

Constipation. Everyone knows prolonged constipation can mean a tumor of the colon, which can be cured with surgery if caught early enough. But did you know constipation can also be a sign of a tumor of the lower spinal cord, which can eventually cause paralysis or death? Sometimes spinal cord tumors will prevent the colon from increasing its motility after meals. This causes constipation, sometimes as an initial symptom.

Diarrhea. Prolonged diarrhea can be caused by food poisoning or colitis, or by infectious and parasitic diseases such as dysentery, shigella, or giardia. But it is also the primary symptom of cholera and Whipple's disease. With cholera—which has been showing up recently in North America—you experience explosive diarrhea, firing out as much as a quart of scorching, watery feces every hour, until you either recover or die of dehydration in a half day of unbearable frothing-at-the-butt agony. People with Whipple's disease envy cholera victims their cushy life. Whipple's disease is a dreadful bacterial infection that occurs mostly in middle-aged white men. It generally shows up as fatty diarrhea. Then it can infiltrate the heart, lungs, brain, spleen, liver, and pancreas. Your joints ache. Your heart gets weak. Your eyesight gets blurry. Sometimes you become spastic, and then you go crazy, and then you die. If it is caught early enough, you can be saved with a lifetime regimen of antibiotics, but sometimes the drugs don't work on the neurological problems. So you feel well enough to entertain, but you serve your guests boiled gophers.

My point is, you might wish to keep an eye on your stools.

Whether we admit it or not, we all sneak a peek into the toilet bowl, at least briefly. It is human nature. The hypochondriac will linger a bit. The human body does not offer too many opportunities for people to examine their biological exudates; a hypochondriac would pass up this chance about as often as a paleontologist would walk past a fibula sticking out of a creek bed.

I asked Dr. Orkin for his advice on what to look for in stools, and he said: "Blood." Then he added, "Also, little squirming things."[11] Other signs are subtler:

Pencil-Thin Stools. A bad sign if they persist over time. If they are unaccompanied by other symptoms, this suggests a narrowing of the intestine, possibly caused by cancer of the rectum or sigmoid colon.

Black Stools. If they are the color and consistency of tar and smell kind of metallic, this can mean bleeding in the upper gastrointestinal tract. Suspect stomach cancer, duodenal ulcers, inflammatory bowel disease, or embolisms or thromboses in the blood vessels of the gut.

White Stools. Often described as being the color of aluminum, persistent pale stools suggest your body is not secreting bile, which gives poop its brown color. You want white stools to be accompanied by pain, because that would

---

11. Want to play a great trick on a hypochondriac? Get a couple of night crawlers and put them in the toilet tank before he goes into the bathroom. The last thing he will see after flushing are two enormous worms swirling down the drain.

probably mean you have gallstones causing an obstruction of the common bile duct; that is treatable by simple surgery. Persistent white stools without pain can mean pancreatic or duodenal cancer, or cancer of the bile ducts.

Maroon Stools. Particularly if they are of pasty consistency, maroon stools suggest bleeding in the lower intestinal tract, possibly caused by colon cancer or diverticulosis. Diverticulosis can sometimes require a colostomy or, in serious cases, removal of the entire large intestine.

Sinkers Becoming Floaters. Yes, there is medical significance to this preschool obsession. If your stools used to sink and now tend to float, it could be a problem. Stool that floats has more fat in it than stool that does not float. Something is causing malabsorption of fat. If you are in pain, it could be an obstructed bile duct or pancreatitis. Without pain, suspect early pancreatic cancer or a diffuse lymphoma of the small intestine.

Gargantuan Stools. This can be one sign of megacolon, in which the large intestine swells up like the *Graf Zeppelin*. The rectum becomes a stern sentry; nothing passes without a struggle. Constipation can be profound, the stools large and hard. Megacolon with constipation tends to indicate a neurological disorder or possibly Chagas's disease, caused by infection by a protozoan. Chagas's disease can eventually cause a total body breakdown, affecting the heart and brain. A final symptom, as listed dispassionately in medical texts after "fever" and "myocarditis" and "ischemic chest pain," is "sudden unexpected death."

No chapter on pooping would be complete without a passage on the passage of gas, and no chapter on the passage of gas would be complete without an interview with Dr. Michael D. Levitt. Dr. Levitt is chief of research at the Veterans Affairs Medical Center in Minneapolis and professor of medicine at the University of Minnesota, and he is the world's leading expert on the subject of farting. I got him on the phone. The very first thing Dr. Levitt told me is that he is famous, and so I worried that he would be a little stuffy, especially when he began listing his credentials.

"I took a fellowship in gastroenterology with Dr. Franz J. Ingelfinger, which is a good name for a gastroenterologist, if you see what I mean. We called him 'the Finger.' He was famous. I realized no one was studying intestinal gas, so you didn't have to do anything particularly good to get published."

I stopped worrying about Dr. Levitt being stuffy.

In a long and distinguished career, Dr. Levitt has published dozens of articles on intestinal gas, including "Floating Stools: Flatus vs. Fat," and what some might consider his masterwork, "Studies of a Flatulent Patient," which chronicles the gas output of one twenty-eight-year-old man who averaged 34 flatulations a day, plus or minus 7, with a standard deviation of 1.[12] A gas chromatograph was used to do detailed chemical analyses. This article was published in the prestigious *New England Journal of Medicine* and includes many footnotes and citations of the work of distinguished doctors, including Michael D. Levitt and Hippocrates.

Dr. Levitt was the first person to figure out a foolproof way to measure the chemical content of intestinal gas: "This is how I got famous," was how he put it. He figured out that since gas is absorbed by the large intestine, and the blood goes into the patient's lungs, "if you sample someone's breath, you can analyze the gases in his intestine."

In other words, we breathe what we fart?

"Well, yes."

Wow.

Dr. Levitt is also the inventor of the Mylar pantaloons, which are baggy, airtight pants that may be worn for purposes of analyzing flatulence. They were sewn by Dr. Levitt's wife, Shirley, who is the Betsy Ross of intestinal gas research. Dr. Levitt's Mylar pantaloons were used to spectacular success in one test of a commercial product, a fart-absorbing seat cushion. Dr. Levitt's tests proved conclusively that this product worked as advertised.

---

12. A normal output is 10 farts a day, with a standard deviation of 5, Dr. Levitt says. "So up to twenty a day can be considered normal." The known medical record is 155 farts in a day.

What is the medical significance of all this?

Passage of gas, Dr. Levitt said mournfully, "is virtually never indicative of serious disease."

So, farting isn't important?

"Right. I am constantly trying to find out why it is important."

But why does he spend so much time studying the field?

"It's a good question. Maybe on my deathbed I will wish I had studied cancer."

The interview was going handsomely, I thought, but something was bothering me. This book is ostensibly about hypochondria, and hypochondria thrives on the fear of serious disease. If farting does not suggest serious disease, why should any of this be of interest to the hypochondriac?

Dr. Levitt tried to help. He said he has conducted studies suggesting that lactose intolerance is a lot of hooey, that people who have been diagnosed as lactose intolerant might well be hypochondriacs.

Big deal.

I could tell Dr. Levitt was holding back, so I said nothing. It's a trick journalists use. Bob Woodward and I are particularly good at it. Sometimes if you just dummy up, your source will get uncomfortable and start babbling to fill in the silence. Sometimes, if he's got a secret, he coughs it up.

Two seconds passed. Four.

"Right now," Dr. Levitt finally said, "the love of my life is sulfur gases produced in the colon." Sulfur gases are what make farts smell bad. "I am in love with the idea that overproduction of gases causes problems."

Problems? What problems?

"It's still theoretical," he cautioned.

Noted.

"Well, ulcerative colitis." Ulcerative colitis is an awful illness that burns and scars your intestines. It holds you hostage to its pain. It can make you a lifelong invalid. Dr. Levitt said that when you analyze the rectal output of people with ulcerative colitis, you find excessive hydrogen sulfide gas, "enough to kill twenty-five mice!"

And?

Hydrogen sulfide is a toxin, he said. Toxins cause disease. His voice got a little theatrical. What if, he said, the hydrogen sulfide is not a *byproduct* of ulcerative colitis? What if it *causes* ulcerative colitis?

Is that possible?

"I am working on it."

But wait. Gas is absorbed into the blood from the intestines. He, Michael D. Levitt, established that many years ago, with the famous breath-fart experiment. Might it be possible that hydrogen sulfide is reabsorbed into the body and causes other diseases?

"It is possible," Dr. Levitt said. "People don't like it when I speculate on that, but I speculate on that."

The phone line crackled. Was it a bad connection, or the electricity of the moment? "Once they are in the blood, gases go to the liver, and then to the lungs, where they are cleared," Dr. Levitt said. Theoretically, he said, they could cause disease to either organ.

What sort of diseases?

Anything, he said, that attacks the liver or the lung.

B-but that could be . . .

"Exactly."

Farts might cause cancer.

Is Death a
Laughing Matter?
Of Corpse Not.

$\mathcal{T}$he meaning of life is that it ends.

You know those signs that say, "Bridge Freezes Before Roadway"? Did you ever wonder what that meant? I found out one day in 1979, when I was driving over a bridge in Lansing, Michigan, in a light drizzle just as the temperature dropped from thirty-three degrees to thirty-two. Instantly, my car was a hockey puck. It spun out and bumped to rest against the guardrail. There was zero traction. Tires wailing, I could not free myself.

I sat there, feeling stupid, when suddenly I saw over my shoulder a City of Lansing truck coming in my direction on the bridge, spreading sand. Good, I thought. Then I realized that the truck, about the size of a big-city garbage truck, was *also* a hockey puck. Shit, I thought. I could see the driver's face. His mouth was agape and his eyeballs were boinging out like golf balls on Slinkys. He was moving about forty miles an hour, barreling right at me. My car was a 1978 Dodge Colt, which is approximately the size of a Saint Bernard.

I opened my car door, stepped out, and began to run. Or rather, my feet began to run. I was on ice. I was stationary. I looked like Fred Flintstone, pre-ignition, feet windmilling in a comical blur, slapping thump-a-thump against the ground, going nowhere.

And then, suddenly, I was going somewhere. I was flying. I blacked out for a moment, and when I awoke I was on my back on the ice. On one side of my body was the truck. On the other side of my body was my car, pulverized into something that looked like a large, smoking Raisinet. Witnesses later told me that the truck hit my car, then my car hit me, and rolled over my body, bouncing once on each side but missing me entirely. The front wheel of the truck was inches from my face. I had no significant injuries.

After the accident, after I realized I had defied death, everything changed. The nighttime sky shimmered with mystery and grandeur. A man could get lost in it, out there in the blackness, sitting cross-legged on the hood of his car, captivated and humbled, oblivious to the cold. A raw tomato, eaten like a McIntosh, was the finest meal a person could want. How could I have not noticed its pebbly, sweet-sour perfection before? A stranger's cigarette butt, hurled from a car window at night, became a thing of beauty, exploding on the road in a tiny, magnificent fire shower. You could taste water, if you tried. You could taste a woman without touching her, if you tried.

This sense of wonder lasted about a month. I tried to hang on to it, but it was no use. Everything returned to normal. You can't summon feelings of mortality. They visit you, stay as long as they wish, and tiptoe away.

Unless you are actually dying.

The first fatally ill person I knew well was Howard Simons, a journalist. Those of you who read the book *All the President's Men* will recognize Howard Simons as one of the principal architects of *The Washington Post*'s exposé of Watergate, the fearless managing editor whose wisdom and unswerving encouragement helped Bob Woodward and Carl Bernstein topple a corrupt presidency. However, those who did not read the book but only saw the hit movie upon which it was supposedly based will instead remember Howard Simons as the cringing swine who looked like Martin Balsam and whose thickheaded skepticism and cowardice almost single-handedly torpedoed the whole project.

Howard Simons was not a bitter man, but he was bitter about this movie misrepresentation, and he had hoped that someday someone would set the record straight in a book. I am sure Howard was envisioning a book with a title like *Principles and Practices in the Ethos of Latter-20th-Century Journalism,* volume VI, *The Watergate Epoch,* as opposed to a book about peeing and pooping. But such is life. And death.

In 1989, Howard started suffering from heartburn and back pain. He went to the doctor, who told him it was advanced pancreatic cancer. In the pantheon of Things Doctors Can Tell You, "advanced pancreatic cancer" is very, very bad. If Things Doctors Can Tell You were, say, popular songs, "Howard, you have the constitution of an ox and should live happily into your hundreds" would be "Johnny B. Goode," by Chuck Berry. And "Howard, I'm afraid you have advanced pancreatic cancer" would be "Muskrat Love," by the Captain and Tennille, as rerecorded by the barking dogs.

In the weeks before his death, I went to Cambridge, Massachusetts, to visit Howard. I had dreaded the visit. What do you say to a dying person?

In real life, Howard Simons sort of looked like Martin Balsam only in the sense that a goldfish sort of looks like a banana. Howard had ice-cube eyeglasses, a nose like an ocarina, and a head of hair resembling the cotton from an aspirin bottle recovered from a plane crash. It was infuriating to me that women invariably found Howard extremely attractive, as opposed to, say, me.

It might have had something to do with the fact that Howard was a lot smarter than, say, me. Howard was one of the smartest people on the planet. He was always right. Not only was he always right, he was always right in a way that was instantly evident to everyone, rendering all previous opinions worthless.

Once, when he was running a fellowship program for writers and editors, Howard brought me and several other big-shot young journalists to interview the man who was emerging as front-runner for the Democratic nomination for president. It was Michael Dukakis. For an hour the governor of Massachusetts regarded us from beneath those flagrant eyebrows and held forth expertly on the great issues of the day. He was never at a loss for words. He never said "um." He had a program for every problem. Once, he fielded a question from a Latino writer and answered in flawless Spanish. It was a masterly performance. We left plainly awed.

In the elevator on the way out, all the savvy young journalists babbled on about how charming and smart and impressive Dukakis had been. Howard listened until everyone else was finished and then said, "Won't win. No sense of humor." Four months later, of course, Dukakis's campaign would collapse in ignominy when the American public discovered he was as dull as a butter knife that had been used to tunnel out of prison. Seeking someone with comparatively more fire and brio and naked animal excitement, the American public chose George Bush.

Howard Simons was only fifty-nine, but he always seemed to be the oldest and wisest person in a room, and this would be true even if the other people in the room were Nelson Mandela, Ruth Bader Ginsburg, and Confucius. An audience with Howard was always just a little bit intimidating. But now that he was dying, the stakes seemed apocalyptic.

There is a tendency to assume that when one is facing death one attains a higher degree of philosophical awareness. Howard Simons getting more philosophically aware would be a fairly scary and maybe even scientifically impossible proposition, like water getting more wet.

I asked Howard if he was angry, and he said, "You mean like this?"—and he looked to the heavens and cried, "Why me, and not Pol Pot?"

Then he smiled and said no, he was not angry.

So I sort of flumphered out what I wanted to know. I do not remember precisely what I said, but essentially I wanted him to show me the world from the unduplicatable perspective of one who is about to leave it, to answer what philosophers have been asking since lumbering prognathous-jawed hominids of the Pleistocene Era contemplated the vastness of the open seas. I asked him to tell me how the imminence of death had altered his perspective on the meaning of life.

This is what he said:

"Mostly, you no longer worry about flossing."

At that moment, to me, Howard Simons was the wisest man on earth.

Two years later, I went to the doctor for a routine cholesterol test. The doctor called the next day and said my cholesterol was fine but that there was something that showed up[1] and he wanted me to stop by the lab on my way to work to take an ultrasound sonogram of my liver.

I said sure, I would arrange for it the next day.

Do it today, he said.

And so I did. It was September 17, 1991, the day I was cured of hypochondria.

The medical procedure was not unfamiliar to me. I had seen it twice before, when my pregnant wife had ultrasound prior to amniocentesis. Amniocentesis is a procedure wherein, to find out if there is anything wrong with the fetus, doctors take an enormous needle and stab it into your belly. (Actually, doctors only made that mistake a few times before they got it right. Now they stab it into your *wife's* belly.)

So there I was, out on the examining table, reasonably calm for a paunchy middle-aged man lying naked in front of a cheerful, businesslike, attractive twenty-five-year-old medical technician who was applying oil to my crotch.

Next she started rolling a computer mouse on my belly, and going, "Mm, mm," and approaching it from all these different directions. Coolly, casually, I asked what she was looking for, as though I really didn't care but just wanted to say something to be polite.

"Usually, looking for tumors," she said.

She was squinting at a computer screen, which was visible to me, too, and there was my liver. Right in the center of it, taking

---

1. If Things Doctors Tell you were, say, foods, "Gene, something showed up in your tests" would be pralines-and-mackerel ice cream.

up maybe a quarter of the screen, was a huge dark elongated mass.

"Um, so what do you see?" I asked, still phenomenally cool.

"I am not permitted to diagnose," she said evasively. It was evidently worse than I thought.

Miss, I said, please, please speak freely.

"I am not allowed to diagnose."

Miss, just answer yes-or-no questions. Do you see that big black mass?

"Yes, I do."

Do you know what that mass is?

"Yes, I do."

If I were your father and you saw that big black mass there, would you be concerned?

"Yes, I would be—"

A maelstrom of horror, self-pity, and ironically, wretched gratitude for this young woman's honesty crashed through my mind. In that flash of perception, I saw my two children, grown, with families I would never know.

"—because my father has had his gallbladder removed, so it would be highly unusual and worrisome if he had grown another one."

Ah.

Anyway, I did not have a tumor. What I had was hepatitis.

There are many types of hepatitis, but the three principal ones are identified by the letters *A, B,* and *C.* Each has its advantages and disadvantages. Hepatitis A has the advantage of being relatively mild, not much more worrisome than a cold, but it has the disadvantage that you get it by eating poop. Feces-contaminated food. I don't know about you, but I think this would bother me a great deal, even years after I recovered. I would never regard a morsel of hamburger quite the same way.[2] Hepatitis B has the disadvantage of sometimes turning you as yellow as a stool pi-

---

2. How much would it take for you to eat your own poop? Would $2,000 do the trick? My dentist told me of a patient with two false teeth who accidentally swallowed his bridge. His choice was to buy a new one for $2,000 or wait for the old one to emerge, clean it up as well as possible, and pop it back into his mouth. He chose option two.

geon but the advantage of typically being transmitted by a wild, carnal lifestyle characterized by indiscriminate sex, intravenous drug use, and/or generally behaving like a rutting jackal. Hepatitis C has the advantage of not being caused by eating poop and not usually turning you yellow. Unfortunately, it has the disadvantage of being the one for which there is no vaccine, no cure, and often no recovery. That's the one I have.

Don't feel bad for me. Hepatitis C is a cool disease. Lots of famous people have had it. Mickey Mantle, for example. King Farouk. Many of these people are currently dead. My point is that I had something serious, which I discovered to be a fantastic cure for my hypochondria.

Actually, it is a fantastic cure for a lot of things. What I learned, basically, is that—to put it as succinctly as possible—you no longer worry about flossing. A few weeks after I found out about my illness, the contractor who built the $16,000 deck in my backyard disappeared shortly before the job was done. Just . . . disappeared, right after my last check had cleared.[3] Prior to my discovering I had a serious disease, my reaction would have been somewhat immature. I would have begun calling this person at 4 A.M., egging his car, sticking a potato in the exhaust pipe, etc. But everything was different now. My view of life had totally changed. So I beat him to death with a baseball bat. I mean, what are they gonna do, execute me twice?

No, the fact is, I let it slide. Now, for those of you dying out there, I would like to warn you that "letting it slide" can become a bad habit. Not bothering to floss can become not bothering to brush one's teeth, and then not bothering to change one's clothes, then not bothering to pull down one's underpants before one goes to the bathroom, et cetera. It is kinder to others to behave as though you are not dying.

You will be reading more about hepatitis C in the years to come, because doctors agree it is very likely the next epidemic. It

---

3. This is not a home improvement book, but while I am on the subject, let me just say that it is not the wisest strategy to pay off a contractor before he completes the job. It is counterproductive. It is like roasting a chicken, seasoning it to perfection, and then attempting to swallow it whole.

is spread by contaminated blood and can stay in your body, undetected, for as long as thirty-five years. Many people who have it today contracted it in the 1960s and 1970s, during the heyday of casual intravenous drug use. I don't know for certain where I picked it up—you can never be sure—but I have a suspicion, based on the fact that I cannot recall precisely where I was, and precisely what I was doing, between December 1968 and June 1971. My clearest memory of that era is discovering in my refrigerator an egg so rancid it stank right through the shell. I was young and callow, but I was not a complete animal. Even at the age of nineteen, I knew how to handle a situation like that. I took the egg, climbed to the roof of my apartment building, and dropped it on a police officer.[4]

Anyway, when you learn you might be dying, you start performing certain mental gymnastics to make yourself feel better. You take refuge in *The World Almanac.* "Hey, in the year 1250, the average man lived to be thirty-eight. I am already *waay* ahead of the game!" You start reading the obituaries, and you take solace from anyone who died younger than you. You can't help it; a school bus crash somehow fills you with joy. The Germans have a hip term for this. It is *Schadenfreude,* and it means taking a subtle, guilty pleasure in the misfortune of others whom you have gassed to death.

It was during this time that I met the man who was to become my personal gastroenterologist, Louis Y. Korman. The Y stands for "Yves." "Yves" does not fit Dr. Korman.[5] "Yves" is as inappropriate for Dr. Korman as, say, "McGeorge" would be to Mr. Buttafuoco. Dr. Korman should be named Hopalong. He is a guy with orange hair who grew up in New York and talks like Jimmy Cagney doing an impersonation of Bugs Bunny.

Dr. Korman is a wonderful doctor, in the sense that he seems

---

4. Also, I attended Woodstock. My roommate and I slept in a tent constructed in the following manner: A tennis ball was placed in the center of a disposable plastic painter's drop cloth and cinched with a rubber band. This was hung from a tree. The corners of the drop cloth were fastened to the ground with forks. These were among the finest accommodations available at Woodstock.

5. Other ridiculously inappropriate names: "Fred" Astaire, "Gladys" Knight, "Humphrey" Bogart.

to know what he is doing, and he has a terrific if somewhat morbid sense of humor. He was the man whose sensitivity I would need to get me through the trying times ahead. Unfortunately, Dr. Korman has the sensitivity of a corduroy condom. Plus, like all doctors, he sometimes dispenses critical information gingerly, as though too much of it could cause harm—as though the patient were a thirsty hummingbird and the doctor were standing there with a fire hose.

Dr. Korman informed me that I had a disease no one knows much about. I asked him how bad it could get before it killed me, and he said, "It would not be productive to discuss that at this particular point in time."

So, I said, "Listen, Doc, just tell me the worst thing that could happen. The worst symptom."

"The worst symptom?" he asked.

"The worst symptom. I want to know. If I know the worst possible symptom, I can deal with anything else."

"Well, that would probably be what we like to call 'feminization.'"

Thank you very much, I said. See, that wasn't so bad. Could you have an orderly clean this up, please?

In order to be diagnosed absolutely, I had to have a liver biopsy. This is a procedure in which a doctor with orange hair sits next to you and makes small talk and tells you to look at the far wall, and you think this is because it is necessary to position your body just so, but then you realize at the last minute that he is bootlegging something he doesn't want you to see. It is, basically, a bayonet.

"You will feel a little pressure now," he says,[6] and stabs you in the side. To say it is the "side" is a little misleading, since he inserts it a few inches into your body. Most men never feel anything enter a few inches into their body, except food. For all I know, women find a liver biopsy pleasurable, but let me just say, as a man, that it feels like an unacceptable invasion, kind of like getting an umbrella inserted in your rectum, then having it

---

6. Food analogy, *continued:* "You will feel a little pressure now" is chicken soda.

opened up and suspended by the handle from a chandelier. Not that I have ever experienced that. Actually, for all I know, women would like that, too.

After your biopsy, you have to lie still for six hours in the hospital's "endoscopy suite," which consists of yourself and a half dozen people who have had a procedure known as an endoscopy. An endoscopy is a routine examination of the lower colon in which doctors give you general anesthesia and then puff your intestines up with air to check for abnormalities. So, after a liver biopsy, you get to spend six hours lying down, contemplating death, in a roomful of people loudly farting themselves awake.

The first thing Dr. Korman told me is that he would recommend, as an option, that I no longer drink alcoholic beverages. He said this the way one might recommend, as an option, not gargling with scorpions.

Prior to this diagnosis, I drank moderately for a journalist, which is to say I would typically fall asleep each night unconscious in my own drool. Stopping drinking proved to be relatively easy, except for wanting to suck my eyes out with a plumber's helper. It is not so much that I missed the alcohol. I did not miss the alcohol. I missed *being soused* from the alcohol.

As a teetotaler, you will think you are getting along just fine, and then one day you will be at a cocktail party, kind of late, and your friend Joel will be standing there with a glass of wine in his hand, surrounded by other revelers, also holding drinks, and it will be their fourth or fifth drink, and Joel will be observing that the great mystery of humankind is not the existence of God but why only humans possess a state of consciousness, and someone else will respond that his dog, Zsa Zsa, has a soul, and someone else will say he has heard that a goose tastes better if it has been strangled to death, and everyone will laugh, and you will want to be there too. But mostly, not drinking is OK.[7]

Hepatitis C is not currently curable, but in some cases it can be controlled. It is treated with the drug interferon, which used to be extracted from baby foreskins but now is synthesized from

---

7. Advice: Nonalcoholic beer is a concession best left unmade. Calling it beer is like calling an aphid a bald eagle.

a bacillus that grows on feces. (Medical science is always making wondrous advances.) Before he prescribed it, Dr. Korman warned me that interferon can have certain side effects. I asked him what they were, and he kind of waffled around and mentioned headaches, and flu symptoms, and a whole web of reported ills. I sighed and said, Look, Doc. The worst.

He said, "The worst?"

Yes, tell me the worst side effect.

"That would probably be the, um, suicide." I do believe Dr. Korman enjoys these little colloquies.

Fortunately, I have been able to handle interferon fairly well. There are certain problems. For one thing, you have to inject it three times a week into your upper thighs. Now, ordinarily, your thighs are not a particularly sensitive part of your body, compared with, say, your tongue or your eyeballs or, if you happen to have them, your testicles. But when you are on interferon, those things might as well be made from bowling-ball rubber because all of the sensation in your body is concentrated in your swollen, aching thighs. You will be sitting in a chair and a cute little three-year-old child will playfully bound into your lap, and you will playfully swat her down with a two-by-four, if one is handy.

But that is the least of your worries. Interferon's biggest side effect is that it makes you tired and irritable. *How* tired and irritable, you ask? Why do you always have to interrupt me? You think I have nothing better to do than answer your stupid questions?

Interferon works by goosing your immune system, which means that, basically, you never get a cold. The cold germs enter your body, but they don't cause symptoms. The odd thing is that every once in a while, without warning, when you are otherwise feeling fine, a single cold symptom will squirm its way through the drug. Because you are unaware that you have a cold, you are unprepared for this. You will be at tea with the archbishop of Canterbury, for example, and you will be declaiming intelligently about Stendhal and the role of a plutocratic society in the changing global climate when you will suddenly hawk up onto his lap a loaf of phlegm the size of a Denver Bronco shoulder pad.

Interferon is still an experimental drug. It has not been

around that long, and there have been no comprehensive studies done on its long-term effects. Dr. Korman warned me about this. He said it is always theoretically possible that this drug, over time, will cause health problems.

"What sort of health problems?" I asked.

"All sorts of things," he said.

"Like . . . a stroke?"

"Could be," he said cheerfully. Doctors love to tell you about potential complications because it takes them off the hook. If they've warned you, they're clear.

"Could it give me tumors?" I said.

"Possibly," he said.

"Enormous worms in my scrotum?"

"Can't rule it out!"

"Could my entire body floop inside out, with a sickening squish, so all my internal organs are just hanging out there like a possum on the highway and people would vomit when they see me and I would have to quit my job and become a carnival freak in Calcutta?"

"The literature isn't clear on that."

Interestingly enough, I have never suffered any actual symptoms from my hepatitis virus itself. My hepatitis virus has spent years quietly doing its job, slaving away, assassinating liver cells, and my liver is still functioning fine. That is the nature of the liver. The liver is not like most other organs, which are small and delicate and highly efficient. If organs were businesses, a kidney would be a tidy French restaurant, with a pastry chef and a *saucier* and a head chef and a maître d' and a small, busy staff of waiters, busboys, and sommeliers, all working together harmoniously to create a daily miracle of art and skill. The liver, on the other hand, would be more like a sanitary landfill staffed by twelve drug addicts and a dog. Now, let's say the hepatitis C virus is a homicidal postal worker with a Kalashnikov assault rifle. Turn him loose in the restaurant, and within a few seconds he will have taken out two or three highly skilled professionals, the delicate balance of jobs will be upset, and the whole restaurant will close up. But send that virus to the landfill, and who cares? A landfill staffed by *one* drug addict and a dog will appear to operate just fine. Sometimes for years. And then, one day, the gases will ignite. It will not be pretty.

The technical name for the process of the eating away of your liver is "cirrhosis," though you have probably heard of it only as "cirrhosis of the liver," since that is the only way journalists write it. "Cirrhosis of the liver" is one of those ridiculous redundancies that journalism is locked into. It is like saying "a heart attack of the heart." But to journalists, "cirrhosis" sounds somehow incomplete or inelegantly shortened. They would no sooner write about just plain "cirrhosis" than they would refer to "Al Einstein."

For the sufferer of hepatitis C, there is no shortage of available terrifying literature. Most of it is intended to be reassuring, but when you get right down to it, there is not much reassuring you can say to someone with an incurable, life-threatening disease. When you try, you sound a little slaphappy and deluded, like an aerobics instructor in a ward for quadriplegics.

I am looking at an article in *Alternative Medicine Digest* about Naomi Judd, the country singer, who has hepatitis C. She tried interferon but stopped using it. She just didn't believe in putting crazy medical stuff into her body. Instead, Naomi treats herself with "milk thistle," carrot juice, vitamins A, B, C, and E, beta-carotene, zinc, biotin, folic acid, selenium, calcium, magnesium, potassium, garlic powder, soy lecithin, niacin, plant sterols, extract of calves' thymus glands, acupuncture, chiropractic adjustment of her spine, progressive muscle relaxation, massage therapy, psychotherapy, morning and evening quiet times, prayer, breathing exercises, yoga, and antioxidants. "I feel strongly about antioxidants," she says. Naomi still has hepatitis C.

Me too. My liver has been damaged. It is possible that at some point in the future I will need a liver transplant to survive. This is not as scary as it might sound. Transplant technology has become so sophisticated that you read in the paper every day about people getting multiple organ transplants; the governor of Pennsylvania recently got a heart, a lung, a liver, a spleen, a pancreas, a kidney, a huge penis, etc.

The main problem is that there aren't enough donors. All over America, perfectly healthy organs are being buried because the grieving public is not adequately informed about how much good their loved ones' organs could do. Often the problem occurs right at the deathbed, when insensitive doctors fail to properly instruct the grieving relative in his options and responsibilities.

Here is a typical hospital room conversation.

Doctor: I'm sorry, we did everything we could.

Grieving Widow: Sob sob sob sob sob.

Doctor: There's just this one teensy little thing . . .

Grieving Widow: Sob sob sob sob. Y-yes?

Doctor: Gene Weingarten needs your dead husband's liver.

Grieving Widow: *Snif.* Who?

Doctor: Gene Weingarten. He wrote this book.

Grieving Widow: So he's the one who made my husband die?

Doctor: Well, in a sense, yes.

Grieving Widow: Give me that liver. I'll *eat* it before he gets it.

Please, don't let this happen to someone you love. Go and fill out your organ donor cards. By the way, while you are at it, specify that you want your liver to go to me, Gene Weingarten, of Bethesda, Maryland. Send me a copy and I will phone you when I get sick, and tell you when you have to kill yourself, and the best way to do so to keep your liver intact. (*Good:* Gunshot wound to head. *Better:* Decapitation by guillotine in hospital emergency room. *Bad:* Drink self to death. *Worst:* Machete through liver.)

I spent a few months recently with Steven T. Mendelson, a thirty-five-year-old Chicago artist who was dying of AIDS. I was helping Steve write his memoirs for *The Washington Post,* and during that time we got to know each other well.

A conversation between an individual who is dying and an individual who is not dying is much more difficult for the relatively healthy person. The relatively healthy person—let's call him Gene—is overwhelmed by the fact that the other person—let's call him Steven T. Mendelson—is dying. It is all the healthy person can think about. It colors every moment. Steve will say something like, "Would you like a cookie?" and Gene will think,

My God, here is this person WHO IS DYING, and all he can think about is my sustenance! He could be consumed by self-pity; ANYONE in his circumstances would be consumed by self-pity. Clearly, this is no ordinary human being. Clearly, this is St. Francis of Assisi!

Meanwhile, Steve will have been holding out the cookie for two minutes. His arm will be getting tired.

He will say, "My arm is getting tired."

And Gene will think, Good Lord, he is suffering a transient ischemic attack, a precursor to a stroke, which is not uncommon in persons with terminal illnesses and frequently manifests itself in a loss of sensation in the arm. I had better act normal, so his final sight in this life will not be a friend recoiling in fear.

And Steve will say, "Look, do you or do you not want the damn cookie?"

And Gene will think, He is feeling hostile. Of *course* he is hostile. He is facing the ultimate indignity delivered by a cold and implacable universe, an ironic, absurdist drama of release without redemption, finality without closure. Gene will think instantly of Dave Barry's definition of a sense of humor: "A sense of humor is a measurement of the extent to which we realize we are trapped in a world almost totally devoid of reason. Laughter is how we release the anxiety we feel at this knowledge." Suddenly Gene will be overcome by waves of rolling mirth, huge crescendos of deep, hearty, thunderous laughter, and he will reach out, weeping with joy and grief and love and fear, and engulf Steve in a gigantic gibbering smothering bear hug, and Steve will drop the cookie and the cat will eat it.

Steve had come home to die in the room he grew up in. On the walls were magnificent, elaborate murals he drew at age thirteen or so. They were of handsome, doe-eyed young men in Lord Fauntleroy costumes. As a boy, Steve wore capes, even at home. Not Superman capes, but brocaded things with crushed velvet. Steve, of course, knew he was gay. His siblings knew he was gay. The meter reader knew he was gay. The only people who did not know he was gay were Steve's mom and dad, who were smart and perceptive and loving individuals unfortunately blinded by PDS, parental denial syndrome. This is the same syndrome that caused parents in the 1960s—my parents, for example—not to realize that their son was stoned when he came home wearing his clothes inside out and fell asleep with his face in the beef Stroganoff.[8]

Anyway, Steven Mendelson loved classical music, especially horrible weepy gothic stuff by Sibelius, and he kept trying to get me to like it, too. He would play this interminable movement of violins and cellos and bassoons and kettledrums—not a decent guitar lick to be found—and then ask me what it made me feel like. The truth was, it made me feel like sticking my head in the toilet and flushing. But Steve was dying! He was reaching out to me in the most intimate of ways. So I didn't say what I really thought. I said the music, um, made me feel real peaceful-like, and, ah, it made me think of eternity and empty, unexplorable voids and the insignificance of our temporal being.

And he said, "Oh. Well, it makes *me* feel orange."

I really, really liked Steve.

One of the last things Steve told me before he died was that he believed in an afterlife. He did not know what it would be: something uplifting, perhaps, or something judgmental and punishing, or something impossibly boring, like an endless game of miniature golf. But he was certain there was something, and he promised, if possible, to return from the dead and furnish me proof. I will know there is an afterlife, he said, if I wake up one morning to find my home tastefully decorated.

Me, I believe that when we die, we go to a place where everything is funny and divine retribution is the rule. Pompous people are compelled to dress like Donald Duck, with a shirt but no pants. The streets are festooned with renowned works of art by LeRoy Neiman and $300 designer shoes by Bruno Magli and ostentatious Rolex watches and Fabergé eggs, but dogs walk around peeing on them. This all lasts about an hour. Then a fat

---

8. Part of the reason my parents never suspected was that I attended the Bronx High School of Science, a nerd mecca. (Motto: "Our Eyeglasses Are as Thick as Sealy Posturepedic® Mattresses.")

guy with a clipboard shows up and starts taking names. I'm not sure what comes after that, but I think it is bad.

Unless you are a fairly old person, or prone to smoking crack while driving, there is a pretty good chance that I will be dead before you will. You may one day see my obit in the newspapers. It will be a modest obit, and because obit writers love irony, it will center on this book and how I gamely predicted my own death, joked about it, won the Nobel Prize for literature, etc. It will no doubt mention my final deathbed words, which I have been planning for years and fully intend to say. They are:

"I should have spent more time at the office."

So. Let's say you are reading the obit and wondering, you know, hey, wait a minute, is there an afterlife? Is there any meaning to all of this? Can ol' Gene send me a signal?

What are you—stupid? I'll be *dead*.

Bibliography

Adams, Raymond D., Maurice Victor, and Allan H. Ropper. *Principles of Neurology* (sixth edition). New York: McGraw-Hill, 1997.

Barsky, Arthur. *Worried Sick: Our Troubled Quest for Wellness.* Boston: Little, Brown, 1988.

Baur, Susan. *Hypochondria: Woeful Imaginings.* Berkeley: University of California Press, 1988.

Bennett, J. Claude, and Fred Plum. *The Cecil Textbook of Medicine* (twentieth edition). Philadelphia: W. B. Saunders, 1996.

Bouchier, Ian A. D., Harold Ellis, and Peter R. Fleming, eds. *French's Index of Differential Diagnosis* (thirteenth edition). Oxford, Eng.: Butterworth-Heinemann, 1996.

Brallier, Jess M. *Medical Wit and Wisdom.* Philadelphia: Running Press, 1993.

Cantor, Carla, and Brian A. Fallon, M.D. *Phantom Illness: Shattering the Myth.* Boston: Houghton Mifflin, 1996.

DeGowin, Richard L. *DeGowin & DeGowin's Diagnostic Examination* (sixth edition). New York: McGraw-Hill, 1994.

Drake, William. *Sara Teasdale, Woman and Poet.* Knoxville: University of Tennessee Press, 1979.

Ehrlich, Richard. *The Healthy Hypochondriac.* New York: Holt, Rinehart and Winston, 1980.

Fuller, Geraint. *Neurological Examination Made Easy.* New York: Churchill Livingstone, 1996.

Gittleman, Ann Louise. *Guess What Came to Dinner.* Garden City Park, N.Y.: Avery, 1993.

Glanze, Walter D., Kenneth N. Anderson, and Lois E. Anderson, eds. *The Mosby Medical Encyclopedia.* New York: Plume, 1992.

Goroll, Allan H., Lawrence A. May, and Albert G. Mulley. *Primary Care Medicine* (third edition). Philadelphia: J. B. Lippincott, 1995.

Gould, George M., and Walter L. Pyle. *Anomalies and Curiosities of Medicine.* New York: Bell, 1896.

Hart, F. Dudley, ed. *French's Index of Differential Diagnosis* (eleventh edition). Chicago: John Wright & Sons, 1979.

Kelley, William. *Textbook of Internal Medicine* (third edition). Philadelphia: Lippincott-Raven, 1992.

Kunz, Jeffrey R. M., ed. *The American Medical Association Family Medical Guide.* New York: Random House, 1982.

Larson, David E. *The Mayo Clinic Family Health Book.* New York: William Morrow, 1994.

Post, George W., et al. *The Cottage Physician.* Empire Publishing Co., 1902.

Rapoport, Alan M., and Fred D. Sheftell. *Headache Relief.* New York: Simon & Schuster, 1990.

Sapira, Joseph D. *The Art and Science of Bedside Diagnosis.* Baltimore: Williams & Wilkins, 1990.

Seidel, Henry M., et al. *Mosby's Guide to Physical Examination* (third edition). St. Louis: Mosby, 1995.

Tierney, Lawrence M., Stephen J. McPhee, and Maxine A. Papadakis. *Current Medical Diagnosis and Treatment* (thirty-fourth edition). Stamford, Conn.: Appleton & Lange, 1995.

Index

abdominal pain, 124–33
  diagnosis of, 126–31
  questions about, 131–33
  referred, 126, 128–31
Adams, John, 32–33
AIDS, 97, 143, 164, 194–96
alcohol consumption, 190
  flushed face after, 70
  Hodgkin's disease and, 121
Alcoholics Anonymous, 112
alcoholism, 29n, 112–15
  self-diagnosis of, 113, 114–15
  signs of, 113
Alice in Wonderland syndrome, 93
alternative medicine, 28–29
Alternative Medicine Digest, 193
Alvarez, W. C., 32
Alzheimer's disease, 71
ameloblastoma, 75
American Diabetes Association, 51
American Journal of Forensic Medicine and Pathology, 172
amyloidosis, 129
amyotrophic lateral sclerosis (Lou Gehrig's disease), 91n
angina pectoris, 110
angioplasty, 109

ankylosing spondylitis, 166
Anomalies and Curiosities of Medicine (Gould and Pyle), 151n
anterior uveitis, 165–66
anthrax, 66
aortic aneurysm, 110, 129
Apley rule, 127
apnea, obstructive sleep, 74–75
apoplexy, 43
appendicitis, 29–30, 127, 130, 154
  fallopian tube vs., 50
  tapeworm vs. 79n
armpit, pain in, 26
arrhenoblastoma, 132n
Art and Science of Bedside Diagnosis, The (Sapira), 119n
arthritis, 141, 143, 154, 166
asparagus, urine smell affected by, 54
Au-Henkind test, 165

Babinski sign, 97
bacteria, 176
  flesh-eating, 52–53
bad breath, 72–73
Barnard, Christiaan, 109
Barry, Dave, 15–19, 195

Bass, Henry E., 169
Batista, Randas, 110
beer potomania, 29n, 113
Behcet's syndrome, 166
Bernstein, Carl, 182
biological weapons, 66
bitrochanteric lipodystrophy, 104n
black stools, 176
blahs, 71
Blumenfield, Hal, 93
Boswell, James, 33
bowel problems, 65, 130, 170–80
   diarrhea, 175–76
   foreign objects as, 172–74
   irritable bowel syndrome, 144,
     175
   stools and, 176–77
   see also constipation; farting
brain, 87, 91–101
   alcoholism and, 113
   central herniation of, 73
   central pontine myelinolysis of,
     42
   infections of, 79, 100
   intelligence and size of, 45
   pineal gland of, 80
   questions about, 99–101
   seizures and, 69, 78
   spongiform, 95–96
   worms in, 79
brain tumors, 64, 71, 78, 79,
     92–95, 99, 108, 167
   déjà vu and, 69
   lipstick on one's teeth and,
     70–71
   optic nerve bulge as symptom
     of, 61
   schwannoma, 67
   sweating as symptom of, 60
   yawning and, 73
breathing, 108, 126, 178, 180
bronchiectasis, 106, 108
Brooker, Philip, 16
burnt match, smell of, 92
Burr, Aaron, 45
Bush, George, 184

calculus, 86
cancer, 54, 60, 68, 70, 106, 108,
     112, 114, 116–23, 130, 147,
     153, 155, 156, 167, 176,
     177, 183–85
   alternative medicine for, 29
   creepiest form of, 122
   cures for, 49, 53
   diagnosis of, 120–21
   doctor's euphemisms for, 86
   farting as cause of, 180
   fig poultice for, 45
   itching and, 68–69
   joke about, 118
   metastatic, 118, 122, 140
   silliest forms of, 121–22
carcinoid syndrome, 70
carpal tunnel syndrome, test for, 24
Caruso, Enrico, 32
Cavett, Dick, 34
Cecil Textbook of Medicine, The
    (Claude and Plum), 104
Cermak, Anton, 131
Chagas's disease, 177
Charles II, King of England, 43n
Chinese restaurant syndrome,
    81–82
chloroma, 121
cholecystitis, 126, 129
cholera, 50–51, 175–76
chronic fatigue syndrome (CFS),
    29n, 144
cirrhosis, 69, 74, 193
Cleveland, Grover, 76
clostridial myonecrosis (gas gan-
    grene), 137
clubbing, fingertip, 105
colds, 34–35, 191
   dire explanations for, 66
   neglected, death caused by,
     57–58
cold sores, 67–68
conception, tranquillity at moment
    of, 45
confabulation, 78
conjunctivitis, 165, 166
   gonococcal, 163–64
constipation, 130, 155, 175, 177
   arsenic treatment for, 45
   of Japanese women, 170–71
coronary artery disease, 105

coronary bypass, 109–10
cor pulmonale, 75
Cottage Physician, The (Post et al.),
    44–45
coughs, 103*n*
    heroin treatment for, 45
crepitus, 139
Creutzfeldt-Jakob disease, 95–96,
    98
Crohn's disease (regional ileitis),
    130–31
Crosby, Norm, 93
cysticercosis, 79

Davis, Eric, 117
death, 45–46, 59, 73, 92, 113,
    140, 143, 155, 156, 157,
    175, 176, 177, 181–97
    abdominal pain and, 129, 130,
        131, 132
    afterlife and, 196–97
    as "bad result," 90
    from cancer, 116, 117, 120, 153
    as "cessation of vital signs," 76
    from heart attacks, 109, 110,
        111
    ironic, 58*n*
    last words at, 77, 197
    neglected colds as cause of,
        57–58
    by pickles, 46
    by suicide, 35, 191
decapitation, consciousness after,
    99
déjà vu, 69
dementia, 43, 71, 143
diabetes, 72, 97, 134, 154
    historical treatment of, 44
    suddenly increased incidence
        of, 51–52
diarrhea, 175–76
diverticulitis, 127, 130
diverticulosis, 177
doctors, 31–32, 37, 41–46, 55–59,
    63, 64, 67, 76, 79, 85, 141*n*
    ancient Greek, 31
    arrogance of, 43–46
    creative euphemisms of, 77,
        83–90

family, 56–58
gastroenterologists, 126–28
goat as fee of, 47
harm done by, 42, 88
Hippocratic oath of, 42
historical quackery of, 43–46, 51
humor in, 160*n*
laissez-faire attitude in, 56–57
misdiagnosis by, 42–43
mnemonic devices of, 99*n*
obstetricians, 150, 151, 153
oncologists, 116–18
on rounds, 85
surgical errors of, 50
Dukakis, Michael, 184
Duvall, Shelley, 99
dyspnea, 37

earlobes, 119
    crease in, 105
ears, ringing in, 67
eclampsia, 155
edema, test for, 109
elephantiasis, 33
embryonal carcinoma, 153
emergency rooms, 75, 111
    screening tests in, 38, 94–95
encephalitis, 37, 62, 73, 79, 166,
    167
    herpes simplex, 100
endocarditis, 104, 106
enemas:
    marshmallow, 44
    turpentine and stinkweed,
        44–45
epididymis, 119
epidural injections, 151
episiotomies, 151
erythema multiforme (Stevens-
    Johnson syndrome), 71
esoneuroblastoma, 74
esophagus, 106, 112, 147
eyelid tics, 22–23, 91, 113
eyes, 61, 127, 158–69, 171
    diagnostic tests for, 164–65, 168
    disorders of, 56–57, 161–67,
        168
    floaters in, 60–61, 164, 166
    medical books about, 163–64

eyes (*continued*)
    objects causing blindness of,
        159–60
    questions about, 168–69
    structure of, 160–61
    surgery for, 162–63

fallopian tubes, 50, 156
farsightedness, 161, 164
fart-absorbing seat cushion, 178
farting, 139, 177–80
    breathing and, 178, 180
    cancer caused by, 180
    through penis, 122n
    sulfur gases in, 179–80
fat, body, 48, 104n, 134–37
fatal familial insomnia, 65–66
fetal monsters, 157
fever blisters, 67–68
fibromyalgia, 143–46
    diagnostic pressure points in,
        144–46
fig poultices, 45, 51
Fixx, Jim, ironic death of, 58n
flesh-eating bacteria, 52–53
floaters, eye, 60–61, 164, 166
floating stools, 177
"Floating Stools: Flatus vs. Fat"
    (Levitt), 178
flushed face, 70
Fox, Henry, 117–18
Freud, Sigmund, 100
frog in stomach, 32

gallbladder disease, 86, 126, 127,
    129, 176–77
gargantuan stools, 177
gas gangrene, 137
George Washington University
    Medical Center, 111
giggle incontinence, 66
glaucoma, 165
God, notable mistakes by, 151n
gonococcal conjunctivitis, 163–64
Greeks, ancient, 31
groin, pain in, 58–59
Guillain-Barré syndrome, 68, 81

Hadrian, Emperor, 105
hair loss, 44

hallucinations, 92–94
Hanot's cirrhosis, 69
Harding, Warren, 43
headaches, 61, 62, 77–82, 121
    cruelest, 82
    environmental causes of, 78–79
    stupid medical names for,
        81–82
    symptom chart for, 79–81
headline, funniest, 157
heart, 106
    cancer of, 122–23
    mitral valve prolapse of, 103–5
heart attacks, 49, 64, 72, 75, 86,
    109–11, 126, 147
heart disease, 75, 102–11, 112,
    134, 154, 155
    diagnostic tests for, 24, 105–6,
        108–9
    ischemic, 110
    neglected colds and, 57–58
    surgery for, 109–10
    thumbs lost to, 104, 105
heel-shin test, 98
Helen Keller Eye Research Foun-
    dation, 159
hemochromatosis, 131–33
hepatitis, 129, 155, 186–87
hepatitis C, 186, 187–97
    interferon treatment of,
        190–92, 193
hernias, 103
herpes simplex virus, 67–68, 100
herpes zoster ophthalmicus, 56–57
hiccups, 64–65
Hippocratic oath, 42
hoarseness, 70
Hodgkin's disease, 68, 129
    alcohol consumption and, 121
Hogg, Thomas, 33
hog slop, blindness caused by, 159
home pregnancy tests, 152–53
homosexuality, 38, 194–96
humerus, 160n
Huntington's chorea, 91n
hyperemesis gravidarum, 155
hypernatremia, 42
hyperorality, 100
hypochondria, 21–40
    books for, 27–29

control desired in, 59
cure for, 24, 55, 105, 185
family crises and, 61–62
famous people afflicted by,
    32–35
increased incidence of, 47–53
irresistible diseases in, 96
knowledge sought in, 59–60
mental factors in, 36–40
origin of term, 31
physical sensitivity in, 125
potentially fatal nature of, 35
referred pain and, 126
self-diagnosis in, 23–24
self-exam for, 24–27
transferability of, 61
validation sought in, 85
hysteria, 44, 94
Hystories (Showalter), 29*n*

ice cream headache, 82
ileitis, regional (Crohn's disease),
    130–31
incontinence, 98*n*
    giggle, 66
infections, 79, 100, 137, 143, 176
inframammary ridge, 119
Ingelfinger, Franz J., 178
insomnia, 65–66
insurance, medical, 32, 47–48,
    133
interferon, 190–92, 193
ironic deaths, 58*n*
irritable bowel syndrome, 144, 175
itching, 68–69

jamais vu, 69
Japanese women, 170–71
jargon aphasia, 93
jaw, 58, 75–76
Joffroy's sign, 165
Judd, Naomi, 193

karate chop to neck, 99
Kentucky, University of, 96
ketoacidosis, 72
kidney failure, 64, 66, 72, 108, 154
kidney stones, 86, 126
kissing, 127*n*
Kluver-Bucy syndrome, 100

Korman, Louis Y., 188–92
kuru, 95
kyphoscoliosis, 108

lachrymal caruncle, 169
lactose intolerance, 179
laughter, 195
    resulting in incontinence, 66
laxatives, 45
leukemia, 37, 68, 129
Levitt, Michael D., 177–80
Lhermitte's peduncular halluci-
    nosis, 93–94
Lileks, James, 92, 118, 119*n*
lipstick on one's teeth, 70–71
liptospirosis (Weil's disease), 81
liver disease, 65, 69, 71, 72, 106,
    126, 129, 185–97
    biopsy for, 189–90
    cirrhosis, 69, 74, 193
liver transplants, 193–94
Lockhart-Mummery, J. P., 174*n*
loiasis, 166
Lou Gehrig's disease (amyotrophic
    lateral sclerosis), 91*n*
lungs, 65, 68, 70, 72, 106, 108,
    147
Lupus, Peter, 99
lupus erythematosus, 26, 129, 143,
    154
Lyme disease, 96–97

macular degeneration, 165, 166
mad cow disease, 95–96
magnesium, dietary, 52
malaise, 71
"Management of Colorectal For-
    eign Bodies" (Sackier), 174
Marchiafava-Bignami disease, 113
Markle sign, 127
maroon stools, 177
marshmallow enema, 44
medical insurance, 32, 47–48, 133
megacolon, 177
melanomas, 120
Mendelson, Steven T., 194–96
Ménière's disease, 67
meningitis, 79, 167
Miami Herald, 13–17
micturition syncope, 122*n*

Minds That Came Back (Alvarez), 32

mnemonic devices, medical, 98*n*

moles, 26
  as malignant melanomas, 120

monsters, fetal, 157

Mortimer, John, 171*n*

Mosby Guide to Physical Examination, The (Seidel et al.), 126–27

Mueller's sign, 24

multiple sclerosis, 60, 66, 67, 86, 89, 97, 154

musculoskeletal problems, 138–146
  behavioral signs of, 141–42
  diagnosis of, 140–43, 144–46
  fibromyalgia, 143–46
  myasthenia gravis, 108, 166
  mycosis fungoides, 69
  Mylar pantaloons, 178
  myxoma, 122

nasopharyngeal angiofibroma, 74

nausea, 71–72

nearsightedness, 161–63, 164

nephritic gingivitis, 72

neurology, 72, 91–101
  diagnostic tests in, 92, 97–98

New England Journal of Medicine, 121, 178

New York Times, 49, 170*n*

nitrous oxide, meaning of life revealed by, 55–56

noncardiac chest pain, 175

nonulcer dyspepsia, 175

Norway, 41–42

nose, 66, 74, 165

nosebleeds, 73–74

nutrition, 52, 131, 186
  asparagus in, 54
  cannibalism in, 95
  deadliness of fruits and vegetables in, 45–46
  eggshells in, 45
  squirrel brains in, 96

Obstetrical Journal of Great Britain and Ireland, 45

o'clock, as term, 55*n*

onchocerciasis (river blindness), 166

organ donors, 193–94

orgasm, headache at, 82

Orkin, Bruce, 172–74, 176

osteosarcoma, 140

Paget's disease, 140

palliative treatment, 85, 89

Pancake, John, 168

pancreas, 65, 68, 112, 130, 147, 177, 183–85

Papua New Guinea, 95

paralysis, 78, 94–95

parasitic diseases, 79, 175

Pasteur, Louis, 48

patellar reflex, 98

Pemberton's sign, 108–9

pemphigus vulgaris, 67–68

pencil-thin stools, 176

penis, 69*n*, 119, 149
  broken chicken bone in, 173
  farting through, 122*n*

pericarditis, 110

peripheral neuropathies, 96–98
  diagnostic tests for, 97–98

peritonitis, 126, 127, 129, 154

Perot, Ross, 147

personality patterns, 39–40

pheochromocytoma, 121–22

pica, 100

pickles, deadliness of, 46

pimples, 53, 119

pineal gland, 80

pins and needles, 68

placebo effect, 39

pneumaturia, 122*n*

poisoning, 72, 97, 175
  ptomaine, 131

polycythemia rubra vera, 80, 129

potato bazookas, 159–60

precocious puberty, 89

pregnancy, 44, 45, 149–57
  amniocentesis and, 185
  birthing process of, 151–52
  bodily changes during, 153–54
  diseases complicated by, 154–56
  fetal monsters produced by, 157
  questions about, 156–57

presbyopia, 168
press coverage, 117, 170
of bad medical news, 49–53
prions, 65
Prokop, James, 91–92
proptosis, 165
Proust, Marcel, 34–35
psychiatric disorders, 100
psychotherapy, 100, 128n
ptomaine poisoning, 131
pulse deficit, 106

radial keratotomy, 162–63
Reder, Anthony, 65–66, 94
reduplicative paramnesia, 93
referred pain, 126, 128–31
Reiter's syndrome, 166
retinitis, 164
ringing in the ears, 67
Rodale, J. I., ironic death of, 58n
Roosevelt, Franklin, 77
Rorschach tests, 100–101

Sackier, Jonathan, 173, 174
saddle nose, 66
Schadenfreude, 188
schwannoma, 67
scientific studies, 147–48
anecdotal evidence vs., 147,
148
of consciousness after decapitation, 99
proliferation of, 48–49
of WWI soldiers with jaw pain,
58
seasonal affective disorder, 29n
Sedgwick, John, 77
seizures, 69, 78
sexuality, 82, 127n
anal autoeroticism in, 172–74
eye problems caused by, 183–84
indiscriminate, 100
Shaw, George Bernard, 41
Shelley, Percy Bysshe, 33
Showalter, Elaine, 29n
Simons, Howard, 182–85
Sjogren's syndrome, 70–71
skin, 60, 68–69, 97–98
sleep disorders, 74–75
insomnia, 65–66

smell, sense of, 54n
hallucinations of, 92–93
Smith, Mark, 94–95
Smith, Roy Bruce, 52
smoking, 92, 147–48
snoring, 74–75
snorting out food, 72
Sound Princess, 171
soy, ill effects of, 52
spatial disorientation, 93
spleen, ruptured, 126, 128–29
spongiform brain, 95–96
Stark, Karen, 102–3, 105
stereognosis, 92
Stevens-Johnson syndrome (erythema multiforme), 71
stiff neck, 76
stools, appearance of, 176–77
strokes, 35, 64, 77, 78, 79, 92–95,
99, 108, 147, 154
"Studies of a Flatulent Patient"
(Levitt), 178
suicide, 35, 191
superstitious behavior, 48n
sweating, 37, 60
symmetry test, 118
syphilis, 86, 167
systemic sclerosis, 24

tapeworms, 79
Teasdale, Sara, 35
teeth, 49, 55–56, 72, 75–76
lipstick on, 70
loose, 58
temporomandibular joint syndrome, test for, 24
teratoma, 122
testicles, 132, 149
epididymis in, 119
swollen, 33
tetanus, 76
cold water cure for, 45
thinking, pathological, 100
thumbs, 104, 105
green, 121
thyroid disease, 78, 108, 155, 165
Tinel test, 24
tinnitus, 67
tip-of-the-tongue phenomenon, 71
toes, proposed names for, 73n

toilet paper squares, 172
toothache, 75–76
tranquillity, 45
transplants, organ, 109, 193–94
Trendelenburg's sign, 143
tumors, 59, 69, 70, 74, 116–23,
    140, 155, 165, 175, 185
  diagnosis of, 120
  hiccups and, 64, 65
  "insidious," 75–76
  normal lumps vs., 118–19
  symmetry test for, 118
  see also brain tumors; cancer
two-point-discrimination tests, 97

ulcerative colitis, 179–80
ulcers, 60, 126, 128n, 129, 176
uncinate fits, 92–93
urination, 44
  fainting during, 122n
  insufficient, 113
  overwhelming anxiety during,
    122
urine, 79, 81
  asparagus in smell of, 54
  blue, 59
  cola-colored, 129
Urised, 59
uvula, 24, 98–99, 169
uvulopalatopharyngoplasty, 75

venereal disease, 33
Venn diagrams, 39–40
Viagra, as killer, 49–50
volvulus, 130

Waldenström's macroglobulinemia,
    74

Washington Post, 49, 170, 182–83,
    194
water intoxication, 113
Weekly World News, 52–53
Wegener's granulomatosis, 66
Weil's disease (leptospirosis), 81
Wernicke-Korsakoff syndrome, 113
Whipple's disease, 175, 176
white stools, 176–77
Wilhelmsen, Ingvard, 41–42
Wolfe, Martin, 38
women, 64, 78–79, 119, 127,
    132n, 139–39, 171
  big fat vs. small thin, 48
  eye shadow on, 168
  historical treatments for, 44–45
  Japanese, constipation of,
    170–71
  middle-aged, diseases of, 69,
    70–71
  smaller brains of, 45
  see also pregnancy
Woodstock, 188n
Woodward, Bob, 179, 182
words on the tip of one's tongue,
    71
World War I, soldiers with jaw pain
    in, 58
worms, 79, 166, 176

xiphoid process, 119
X-ray Specs, 168–69

yawning, 73

Zangara, Giuseppe, 131
Zappa, Frank, 171–72
Zimmerman, Lorenz, 159

About the Author

Gene Weingarten (1951–) has been a writer and editor at *The Washington Post* since 1990. Before that he was a reporter for the *Detroit Free Press*, an editor at the *National Law Journal*, and the editor of *The Miami Herald*'s *Tropic* magazine, which he helped lead to two Pulitzer Prizes. In 1988 he was a Nieman Fellow at Harvard University. This is his first book.